MAY -- ...ot

Housing, Feeding,
Socialization

...raphs
...-Bridges

BARRON'S

C O N T E N T S

WHEN PARROTS NEED NEW HOMES

Many, probably most, resale parrots adjust superbly in second homes. Others may go through several homes before finding the right one.

Tim and Bobbie Carter knew nothing about parrots. They knew dogs, and they knew that dogs were overpopulated, so each time they wanted a dog, they adopted one from an animal shelter. They were careful; they didn't adopt just any dog. They had wonderful experiences and wonderful dogs.

When it came time for a parrot, it was only natural that they would look for a parrot that recently had lost its home. As they looked at baby parrots in stores, they asked many questions and accumulated a great deal of information. They found many birds in need of homes. From their years with dogs, the Carters knew that an experienced pet comes with behavioral baggage, so they read everything they could find about the behavior of companion parrots.

Six months later, through the newspaper, they found Cosmo, a two-and-a half-year-old blue-and-gold macaw. They paid less for a bird,

This Goffin's cockatoo was considered a problem bird in her old home. In her new home, she is a treasured family member.

a cage, a free-standing perch, and half a carful of accessories than they would have paid for a newly weaned hand-fed macaw.

Ten years later, Cosmo is a dream bird. His guardians proudly proclaim him the perfect parrot. He is vocal but screams infrequently and at expected times. He likes to talk loudly to new toys, and he stretches out one wing in a macaw salute whenever someone he likes enters the room. He is a delightful and charming companion.

Cosmo's first family, who lived with him less than two years, had a different story, however. The family members thought Cosmo was noisy, nippy, and messy, not to mention mean and vindictive. Finally, when he chewed the frame off a window while they were away on vacation, they decided to find him a new home.

Like thousands of other parrots that are resold for a fraction of their baby value, Cosmo himself was not the problem. His first family was simply unprepared. They didn't know how to teach Cosmo emotional or behavioral independence or how to accommodate his natural behaviors. When they realized that he needed

Should I Change Killer's Name?

Whether the bird is called Killer, Freddie Kruger, Booboo, Hey You, or just Stupid, a parrot may need to be rescued from a horrible name as well as from horrible care. But what happens if the bird's name is changed?

Parrots form strong associations between words or sounds and the situation in which they were heard. This ability allows them to use words at times consistent with their meanings. Name association is so strong that a parrot might continue for many years to say its old name when stressed or become stressed when it hears its old name. If the bird was in an unhappy situation, using the same name can keep the bird in the same "state of mind" and related patterns of behavior. A radically different name can help the bird discontinue past associations.

If the bird was happy in its old home, continued use of the same name can perpetuate its positive behavior. If the bird came from happy circumstances, the transition is easiest if the new name sounds a little like the old one: Coach for Roach, Lover for Killer. Most parrots easily learn any new name that is used frequently.

Even in a well-adjusted bird, a foul name can stimulate human responses that the bird responds to unfavorably. Sometimes changing to a name that people respond to more positively stimulates improvement in the bird's responses. If the bird enjoys your company, it may learn to use its new name to initiate interaction, even if it never learned to say its name before.

more than they could give, he was moved to a back room. There, in isolation, his wild behaviors were free to develop. He began trying to fill his needs in the ways that came most naturally: screaming, chewing, and nipping.

Cosmo and his new flock, which now includes an umbrella cockatoo and a red-lored Amazon, have established successful relationships. Dale and Bobbie volunteer, helping others find, rehabilitate, and adopt displaced parrots. They firmly believe that it's better to buy a second-hand parrot than a newly weaned one.

Are They Problem Birds?

Life's changing circumstances can affect even the most determined person's ability to keep a beloved companion animal, but there's more to it than that. A trip through any humane shelter will reveal that many animals are there because of natural behaviors that were perceived as problematic. Likewise, many parrots are given up because of misunderstood or poorly accommodated natural behaviors.

Most parrot books now available deal with the socialization and care of newly weaned or very young human-raised birds. The resocialization of previously owned parrots is generally different, and it varies more from bird to bird. So, just as social pressure in the 1990s created a need for *Guide to a Well-behaved Parrot* and *Guide to Companion Parrot Behavior,* there is a need now for a book about second-hand parrots. *Guide to the Second-hand Parrot* is a supplement, not a replacement, for those behavioral texts.

Any parrot, whether it's coming into a first or a subsequent home, needs guidance to fit into an already formed family unit or flock. Without guidance, annoying natural behaviors may become more than the group or any one of its members can bear. Inappropriate training can worsen problems. Unintentional reinforcement and unintentional neglect can lead to biting, fearfulness, excessive screaming, and other difficult-to-live-with behaviors.

Interaction and Independence

One bird may be so interactive that it can do nothing without human assistance. Another may be so independent that it prefers not to feel, hear, or see a human. A successful companion parrot learns both interaction and independence.

Many birds lose their first homes because they never became emotionally and behaviorally self-sufficient. Especially, baby cockatoos and macaws may have been held and cuddled constantly when humans were present. If there were several people in the home, the bird may have become totally dependent on humans for every activity, instead of developing exploratory and independent behaviors. This is a common problem for baby cockatoos, which can learn to manipulate humans with powerful vocalizations.

Wild Bird, Wild Behaviors

Some behaviors cannot be eliminated, but they can be accommodated or made less offensive. For example, chewing is normal behavior for these (mostly) cavity-breeding creatures, which carve their nests from tree trunks. It's unrealistic to expect a parrot to care about the difference between a scrap of lumber and an antique clock. A parrot must be constantly supplied with acceptable chewable material.

Parrots are not spayed or neutered like dogs and cats. Consequently, a parrot may lose its home because it develops grooming, vocal, territorial, or other behaviors related to pressure to breed. Those natural instincts must be handled with sensitivity and understanding. Most parrots need at least a little behavioral training in order to fit into most human environments.

A parrot may lose its home for any number of reasons, including personal tragedies of the family or relationship problems between the bird and the family members. With patience and guidance (sometimes a lot of patience and guidance), most of these birds will blossom into their own version of Bob or Cosmo. The purpose of this book is to shed light on the common problems of second-hand parrots and the noble humans dedicated to bringing out the best in them.

WHAT KINDS OF BIRDS ARE AVAILABLE?

Over a six-month span—a reasonable time for reflection and study before assuming responsibility for a long-lived species—there will be at least 30 or 40 types of birds offered for sale in a mid-sized urban area. Usually, about half of them are under two years old.

Domestic Parrots

Radically improved behavior is possible at any age; however, parrots are most docile and trainable if socialization begins before breeding age. A hand-fed bird is usually more social and will bond better with humans than a parent-raised bird.

Most parrots adapt readily when moved to a favorable environment. A new beginning in a new home can bring radically improved behavior almost spontaneously. Established behaviors can be changed more easily outside the environment in which they developed.

Some things can be easily learned at an older age; others cannot. For example, many birds that bite can be trained not to bite. Talking is another matter. If you want a talking bird, buy one that already talks. Adopt a shy bird with caution. Many shy parrots are genetically programmed to be shy. Fearfulness is usually more difficult to change than aggression.

Look for a parrot that has been merely neglected, rather than over-nurtured or abused. A neglected bird may be aggressive or frightened (or both). An over-nurtured bird may have been reinforced in socially and physically destructive behaviors.

There are usually many opportunities to adopt young cockatoos under two years of age. These birds may have developed attention-demanding behaviors, some of which resolve spontaneously with the home change and with strategies for developing independent behavior. Some of these birds can be extremely entrenched in their behaviors, however, and they respond more slowly to efforts to establish independence.

Breeding-age hand-feds also have good companion potential, as long as human expectations are reasonable. A teenaged bird won't act like a baby again. Like any other mature parrot, it eventually will go through fluctuating—usually seasonal—cycles of behavior.

Macaws represent a large portion of the parrots looking for second homes. Many people are not prepared to meet their needs for chewing and attention.

The improved environment of the new home usually brings improved behavior that can be reinforced. There is often a period of adjustment similar to the "Honeymoon Period" experienced by newly weaned parrots in their first home. The initial harmony may be brief. If you quickly and consistently reward each desirable behavior as it appears, the behaviors that cost the bird its first home may not reappear.

Wild-Caught Parrots

When the importation of birds into the United States ended in the early 1990s, there was concern that breeders would be unable to meet public demand for parrots. Domestic aviculture, buoyed by the accessibility of wild-caught breeding stock and amazing advances in avian medicine, was more than equal to the task of providing birds.

The numbers exploded. In the 1960s, 1 in 12 homes house a pet parrot. That statistic jumped to 1 in 6 by the end of the century. There is now a burgeoning population of older parrots. As the humans caring for those birds also grow older, the number of second-hand parrots continues to grow.

Many of these wild-caught parrots, including Moluccan, Goffin's, and Umbrella cockatoos; Quakers; and lories, were captured rather than exterminated as agricultural pests in newly developed agricultural regions. Many others, including eclectus parrots, continue to be trapped and transported on new roads built to accommodate logging in the rain forests.

Many of the imported birds, such as Amazons, macaws and Moluccan and Umbrella cockatoos, are extremely long-lived. Resale wild-caught parrots continue to be available.

Any legally-imported wild-caught parrot in the United States was hatched by 1992.

Although tamed wild-caught parrots sometimes don't learn to say words, they can be charming companions in their own bird-talkin' way. For a patient person, older wild-caught birds can offer good companion potential even if they were previously unsocialized. The bird simply might never have met a human it liked. If you have a way with birds, the bird may like you. Many allegedly untame older birds become spontaneously tame in new homes. One can hope for that, but not expect it. If the bird takes food from your hand and eats it the first time you meet, you have a good chance of being able to befriend it.

If the bird tolerates handling, the bond might be improved by holding it for long periods during the first few days or weeks in your home. That increases the bird's trust without, as it might with an over-nurtured hand-fed bird, creating excessive dependence.

Wild-caught parrots may be occasionally available through adoption programs of aviculture clubs. Some tamed, wild-caught parrots bite less and demand less time and attention than many of their domestic cousins. Many former breeder parrots adjust superbly as companions.

Found Pets

A lost companion parrot is usually hungry, thirsty, and carefully searching for a friendly human. If it fails to find one, a free-flying parrot may become established, or naturalized, in an urban environment. Although naturalized parrots usually represent no threat to agriculture or native species, they are in constant danger. Captured birds found living wild may be available from humane societies and animal control authorities in some states. Wild-hatched baby Quakers are freely available in Florida and Texas, but naturalized escapees are protected in many states.

A recaptured companion parrot may be very hungry and may spend the first few days eating, while you constantly refill the food bowl. The bird may prefer seed, but this period of panic eating may be an excellent opportunity to introduce it to unfamiliar foods.

The "Perfect" Imperfects

Whether we call them "imperfects," the old-time aviculture term for birds with physical anomalies, or "differently abled birds," this group contains some of the most cherished companion parrots. They have survived injuries resulting in disfigurement. They may be available at no cost or in exchange for a contribution to their medical expenses.

In some, the damage is cosmetic; in others, the injuries make it difficult for the bird to function. The deformities may be congenital or the result of accidents related to flying indoors. They may include burns on toes, feet, or legs (from landing on a hot stove, fireplace, or cooking pot), broken wings (from flying into ceiling fans, windows, or other objects), or beak injures (from toy or cage accidents).

Most physical imperfections require no special housing or equipment. Loss of one toe or toenail doesn't interfere with a bird's ability to function normally. Severe imperfections, however, may require handling, dietary, or environmental accommodations such as padded surfaces, flat-topped perches, and cages with ladders. A bird with no feet can adapt to a

Scarlet, the Found Macaw

The caller said that there was a huge red bird, bleating like a baby goat, hanging upside down in the aspen tree beside his home. It was a beautiful young scarlet macaw—hungry, thirsty, and lost. The bird came immediately to the first human she could reach. She bit me hard a few times as I walked her into the nearest house. The bird's human family was never found, in spite of weeks of posters and newspaper advertising. There were rumors in the neighborhood that they didn't want her back.

During Scarlet's first few days in my home, it was easy to see why someone might throw her out the window. Her favorite game was an arm-bruising nip, followed by a loud "Ouch!" and even louder laughter. She was given to extreme screaming in 15- and 20-minute bursts. She bit anyone wearing a garment with buttons unless she was allowed to break a button or two.

Scarlet was dehydrated and semi-starved. She wouldn't eat. The first two weeks I had to hand feed her warm baby parrot formula which she slung all over the kitchen several times daily. Within a month, she was eating regular Harrison's Bird Diet and other offered foods. Within six months, she was a friendly, interactive bird. With just a few repeated games (a little silliness as cooperation patterning) including the use of *"Peekaboo!"* to replace attention-demanding vocalizations, Scarlet became an easy-to-live-with companion. She still loves seeing strangers jump away from a bluff stab, and she still bites some people who won't let her break buttons.

Older parrots can form strong, loving bonds in their new homes.

This red-tailed African grey has adjusted well to the loss of one wing and he enjoys a quality life as a quality companion.

Just because a baby parrot is perfect when it comes to a new home doesn't mean it will stay that way.

Natural behaviors such as chewing or vocalizing create problems until the bird learns to express them appropriately.

A new member of the household may not be immediately embraced by the other residents.

Young Cockatoos are known for being "cuddly," but often lack the skills to entertain themselves when they are not being held.

padded box if the sides of the box are short enough to see over. A bird that loses all or part of its beak may require hand-feeding for a time and adjustment of its diet to assist independent eating.

Many obviously happy birds survive without an eye, keel bone, wing, or foot. Some of them would not have survived in the wild, but, having recovered from the initial injury, they are fully capable of continuing life as a pet. Even birds that have lost important skills such as the ability to walk, fly, climb, see, or eat independently have become—in the right home—happy, successful companions. Imperfects often develop extremely accommodating personalities.

The Bereaved Parrot

A wild parrot is in trouble if it loses its flock. A companion parrot may react adversely to loss of a flock, even if the previous flock was neglectful and abusive. There may ensue a period, usually no more than a few days or weeks, of silence or withdrawn behavior. A parrot that loses a beloved companion may call or continue looking for that favorite bird or person; it may even stop eating for a while. Likewise, a parrot may mourn, call for, or seek a recently deceased household pet. Do what you can to sensitively encourage the bird to move around. Delicious, healthful foods can help a parrot through bereavement. Play lots of happy music.

The new humans should not feel discouraged if the bird fails to immediately "appreciate" the things being done to accommodate it. Some things take time.

No home is immune to the type of tragedy that leads to a pet's need of a new place to live. Protect your birds from the stress and depression associated with losing a loved one. Keep a written record of each bird's diet, preferences, dislikes, vocabulary, veterinarian, groomer, behavioral consultant, pet sitter, boarding facility, and other service providers, and any idiosyncrasies that might prevent a successful transition. The existence of a second or "co-parent" home (see page 86) that can become a permanent home at some future time is ideal. If the bird is already well acquainted with the new human(s) and new permanent home, then the transition is easier. The bird's routine should remain as close as possible to what it was before the loss.

Make arrangements well in advance and keep the information updated. Be sure to make financial provision for the bird's needs. If there is no funding or subsidy accompanying the bird, anything can happen in the hands of well-meaning, but inexperienced family or friends. If there is no provision for the bird in the guardian's will, the bird might wind up in a shelter or worse.

Aviary Birds

Just as some birds prefer to live with humans, other birds prefer to live with birds. A bird may be so bonded to its wild roles, so intent on its own agenda, that it is completely unable to live with humans. Every moment in the company of humans can be stressful to such a bird. This situation is more common among wild-caught birds, lost pets, and parent-raised domestics than in hand-fed domestics. Every effort should be made to provide the bird with as natural an environment as possible and to shield it from contact with humans. Many birds of this type are past breeding age, incom-

Who's the Parrot Trainer?

Paula was proud of Inigo, her second-hand African grey. Although he'd come with a heavy duty screeching problem, a few months of careful attention resulted in a bird that was the envy of her friends. When Paula moved in with her new husband, Hal, the bird's old bad habit popped up again. She tried the tactics she'd used before, but this time they didn't work.

Inigo wanted Hal's attention but could get it only by screaming at ear-shattering volume. Hal wouldn't answer the bird's more quiet "Hello's." He simply wasn't a "bird

person" and didn't want to interact with a parrot.

Hal wanted Paula to train the bird not to scream, but this was an unrealistic expectation. A parrot is a family project, even if there's only one person in charge of cleaning, feeding, and supplying entertainment for the bird. For better or worse, everyone in the home contributes to the bird's behavior. Paula and Hal had to work together to nurture good behavior and discourage the bad. Fortunately, as a team, they were able to restore golden silence to their new family home.

patible with available mates, infertile, or mate-abusive. Large flights of similar types of birds can help keep these birds happy.

Few private individuals have the resources to provide long-term care for groups of aviary birds. Unless a substantial trust can be provided, the best place for these birds is probably a secure, well-established sanctuary organization. There is probably a waiting list for placement of this type, and anyone expecting to surrender a long-lived bird with little or no potential for adoption should be prepared to make a donation—sometimes a considerable sum—for the bird's future care.

The Rest of the Story

A second-hand parrot can be an excellent choice as a first bird. Be especially careful if

you already own birds. A second-hand bird can bring diseases and annoying behaviors with it. Quarantine procedures (see page 50) should be observed. The resident flock will be quick to copy any behaviors that get attention, so be careful not to reinforce anything annoying. Adopting any bird—second-hand or baby—is a long-term commitment that requires time and patience. Most mistakes occur when the decision is made out of pity or on the spur of the moment. If an immediate rescue is unavoidable, you might buy or accept a bird and donate it to an adoption program.

Avoid expectations: Every parrot has similarities to every other parrot, but the delight of all parrots is their individuality. Each bird is a distinct character, with likes, dislikes, and, sometimes, amazing idiosyncrasies.

WHAT ABOUT A SECOND-HAND PARROT?

Sometimes the most wonderful relationships develop suddenly and unexpectedly. A parrot doesn't always come into a home by choice, as parrots are passed in families from one generation to another, and lost birds find new humans. In that case, you get the bird that comes to you.

If you decide to get a second-hand parrot, there are many choices and many reasons to be selective. Look for chemistry, a thunderbolt of attraction between bird and human. Reduce the risk of the bird's having to find yet another home by being realistic about your home and your family's abilities to accommodate a particular parrot.

How Much Does It Cost?

Most parrots come with a price tag. A second-hand parrot advertised in the newspaper generally costs less than one available through a retail or adoption facility. Expect to pay more whenever a bird is placed outside its home for boarding or care while seeking a new home. If

There is a number of factors that you need to take into consideration before adopting a parrot, like this rose-breasted cockatoo.

an organization has rehabilitated a bird with behavioral or medical issues, it should be able to document the bird's physical condition and provide recent medical records.

The chart on page 19 lists estimated costs to accommodate a bird. The lowest number is the absolute minimum expense, for a small, healthy bird with complete medical records. The lowest number also presupposes a resourceful person with time to bargain-shop, plan, and make some accessories. The higher number is the minimum expense for a modest set-up for a large macaw or cockatoo, healthy and with medical records. Of course, you may select more elaborate accessories, including specialized air filtration and cleaning equipment, which are not included in the cost of the bird. Homemade toys and perches are inexpensive, but they require time and creativity to make.

Whether the bird has bonds in its original home or forms them during rehabilitation and foster care, additional stress is placed on the bird each time it changes homes. Although direct placement might be easier on the bird, sometimes it is harder on the human or avian members of the new "flock," because birds coming directly from homes where problematic behaviors developed can bring those behaviors with them.

Compatibility Issues

As with any other long-term responsibility, consider how much time and patience you have. Be realistic. If you've lived with a bird, you're more likely to understand what is involved. If you haven't lived with a bird, offer to board one for a few weeks.

Make a list of things you most want in a parrot and a list of things you don't want. Take a look at the section on expected characteristics of the different species in Barron's *Guide to Companion Parrot Behavior*. It's probably more important to eliminate a species that might be incompatible—for example, a species with powder, a protective dust-like coating present in some birds, including cockatoos, cockatiels, and African greys, in a home where a human is allergic to dander—than to preselect a particular type of bird.

Consider the sound tolerance of housemates and neighbors. If you have plenty of time, tolerance, and space, you might choose a cockatoo, Amazon, macaw, or African grey. If time, tolerance, and space are limited, you might want something more easily accommodated, perhaps a small African parrot, Quaker, conure, cockatiel, or budgie. Most parrots have similar natural behaviors—calls, chewing, territorial needs—that can develop into what some humans might call problem behaviors.

Your Present Flock

If you already have birds, each new addition must be considered carefully. Adding parrots where there are already parrots can cause complications. Although one Quaker or conure may be a joy to live with, adding another often increases wild behaviors in both. Both may become less tame and more noisy. Birds that are similar tend to join together in their vocaliza-

Paco Makes a Choice

Paco, a 20-year-old Lilac-crowned Amazon, outlived his long-time human companion and needed a new home. The bird appeared unhappy in his foster home and refused to eat for several days. He didn't vocalize and wouldn't interact with any of the volunteers or potential adopters who came to visit. Paco had a clean bill of health, but still ate little and had not spoken a word, though he was reported to have a huge vocabulary.

On the tenth day in the foster home, Ed and Rebecca came to see Paco, to consider adopting him. Paco was sitting on the play gym on top of his cage when the couple entered the room. As soon as he saw Rebecca, the colorful little Amazon jumped from the top of the cage onto her shoulder. Then he let out a long, loud wolf whistle and asked excitedly, "For Paco?"

Rebecca cuddled the bird and tickled his belly as the parrot cooed and purred. Ed greeted Paco, who answered with a friendly "Hi there."

Paco has been a beloved member of their family ever since. Rebecca reports that he still asks, "For Paco?" whenever he sees something he really wants!

Cathy Isbel

tions. Whereas a grey might let an Amazon's scream go unanswered, the calls of another grey, a Poicephalus, or another bird with a similar high-pitched call might be answered with great volume. Cockatoos love to scream and display to each other. Macaws prefer to have the last word. Amazons vie to see who can be the loudest. Male parrots of similar types may display and vocalize, even if they aren't the same species. Any bird can introduce bad habits. If the new bird gets attention for unwanted behaviors, the resident birds may mimic.

The Bird's Potential Life Span

The chart on page 22 gives a general idea of how long most common companion parrots can live. This is the maximum estimated life span. Like humans, not all parrots die of old age.

The chart also lists the approximate minimum age at which intrusive breeding-related behaviors such as calling and territorialism tend to appear. Many parrots are capable of reproducing before this time, but problematic behaviors related to pressure to breed don't usually dominate the bird's repertoire of behaviors immediately upon sexual maturity.

Other Pets and Children

Some dogs are obviously predatory, others are not. Comingle parrots and dogs with great care. Dogs can be more dangerous than cats to parrots. Cats often stalk small, active birds but not larger, more stolid ones. Unsupervised ferrets are more problematic than cats, because some ferrets will go for any bird, no matter how large.

Most larger hookbills, especially cockatoos, have trouble fitting into homes that provide

Minimal Set-up Costs

Cage	$20–$600
Manufactured perches and play gyms	20–200
Veterinarian (if the bird is healthy)	40–150

Ongoing Monthly Expenses

Food, including fresh and formulated diets	$10–$60
Toys and chewable perches	6–60

in-home day care for small children. Invasive noises such as fireworks, construction, or frequent sirens can instill terror in a bird and destroy its sense of safety.

Some sensitive humans may be unable to tolerate normal parrot mess or normal parrot sounds. Some people cannot abide the occasional nips, bites, and scratches inflicted by a self-motivated companion animal that has toenails and something resembling a can opener on its face. Even the best-socialized bird may occasionally nip.

Evaluating the Individual

Carefully examine a bird before deciding whether to buy it.

✔ You should be able to feel the central edge, but not the sides, of the keel bone down the center of the breast. The tissue on each side should feel firm and well-fleshed.

✔ The eyes should be clear and shiny, interested, willing to make contact.

✔ The nostrils should be clear of discharge. Breathing should be uniform, with no audible

The malformed beak and eye on this wild-caught white-fronted Amazon are scars from an avian pox infection.

While the bird is no longer a health threat to other parrots, the beak will need regular professional grooming for the life of the bird.

click, although a pionus may wheeze when stressed.

✔ The beak should be symmetrical and not excessively long for the species. Ridges starting under one or both nostrils and continuing down the beak are a sign of chronic sinus infection.

✔ Examine the feet for swollen joints or sores on the bottoms. The feet should open and close and have two toes forward and two toes back. Very fat feet or toes may indicate obesity.

✔ One or two missing toenails are usually insignificant. Sometimes special accommodations must be made if two or more toenails or toes are missing.

✔ There should be no feces caked around the vent.

✔ The droppings should be well formed and have three distinct parts: feces (solids), urates (whites), and urine (clear liquid).

✔ Don't be concerned about an occasional tiny damage line running straight across the long wing or tail feathers (stress bar), but be wary of a bird with multiple stress bars on each feather, which might be a sign of illness.

✔ Feathers are optional. Many second-hand parrots come without them. Sometimes they grow back. Disposition is much more important than appearance, but understand that poor feather condition could be an indication of illness or malnutrition.

✔ New feathers growing in should be little sharp spikes or little straws with healthy feathers coming out of the end. Avoid birds with rounded or clubbed pin feathers, which are a sign of serious illness.

✔ Have copies of the veterinarian's records faxed to your avian veterinarian. If you're dealing with a rehabilitation organization, it may

Parrots who lack the skills to entertain themselves can learn them from watching other parrots.

have already done tests. If the bird is coming directly from its previous home, try to have it examined by a veterinarian before making a commitment to take it.

The Only Bird

Although parrots are highly social creatures, they are also mostly monogamous. Consequently, many companion parrots appear to prefer a primary relationship with a particular human, as a kind of mate. Possibly that explains why solitary parrots can develop very

Due to their longevity, many types of wild-caught parrots are still available. Red-lored Amazons were popular imports.

Sam and Liz

My blue-and-gold macaw, Sam, came to me after 12 years in her previous home. I don't know Sam's history, except that she is an import, and this was not her first home.

Adopting an adult parrot is not always easy. I made mistakes with her in the beginning, and it took time for us to learn to trust each other. It took us a couple of years to work through some issues. That was almost 30 years ago, however, so it hardly matters now. A long-term relationship like ours is similar to a marriage in some ways. We have had rocky periods, but we muddled through. Some days she aggravates the daylights out of me, until I remember that she's been putting up with me for as long as I've been putting up with her—which is quite a feat!

Estimated Attainable Life Spans of Companion Parrots

	Attainable Life Span	Breeding-related Behaviors Appear
Budgies	6–15	6–12 months
Lovebirds, parrotlets, Brotegeris	10–20	1–2 years
Cockatiels	10–25	1–2 years
Conures, Quakers, ringnecks	15–35	2–3 years
Lories	8–25	1–3 years
Poicephalus, pionus, caiques	15–30+	2–6 years
Eclectus	20–30+	1–4 years
Mini-macaws	20–35+	2–5 years
African greys	20–40+	4–6 years
Amazons	25–80+	4–6 years
Macaws	40–80	5–8 years
Cockatoos	30–80+	5–10 years

interactive personalities, with large vocabularies and cooperative habits. Those benefits naturally accrue when an only parrot and its human spend more time together.

The Multiple-Bird Home

Social dynamics can benefit both the flock and the new bird. Although parrots can teach each other bad habits, they can share positive lessons as well. A second-hand parrot in a new home may not know how to play with toys. It may eat only seeds or be fearful of anything new. Watching and listening to the other flock members eat, play, talk, and sing encourage the new bird to become more flexible, increase its vocabulary, and compete for the attention of humans. A parrot that has come from a multiple-bird home where it felt secure with the flock of other parrots and humans should thrive in another such household. Occasionally, individual birds get extremely jealous and refuse to share human company without putting up a fight. Obviously they would not be a good choice for a house with an established flock.

Should I Take In a Parrot Temporarily?

It's becoming apparent that there may be more parrots needing homes than there are homes to accommodate them. When we stumble upon a bird in unhappy circumstances, it's tempting to think about taking it in temporarily. If there are no other birds in the home, then risks are minimal. If there are others, then the well-being of the established birds must have top priority. Carefully consider these elements:

✔ Should I buy a bird I don't intend to keep?
✔ Can I afford adequate housing?
✔ Is there a disease threat to established birds?
✔ Are there unwelcome behavioral issues?
✔ Can I afford medical care for a bird I don't intend to keep?

Be careful. Consider how many birds you have time to interact with and how many cages you can clean. It's easy to be overwhelmed before realizing how much is too much.

Staying Together Through Thick and Thin

No matter how bird-centered a particular family is, there will be times when the bird's needs cannot come first. No matter what the changing circumstances—marriage, pregnancy, divorce, illness, bankruptcy—there will be times when humans must tend to their own affairs, sometimes to the exclusion of the bird.

There's a real temptation to believe that it might be better for the bird if it moved to another home. Unfortunately, that is not usually the case. Often the new home is less dedicated to the bird than the old one and more likely to pass the bird on if there is trouble. Moreover, when a parrot loses a flock or a family unit, it instinctually understands that its life is threatened. This reaction is genetically programmed, derived from the bird's wild ancestors. Many companion parrots emotionally self-destruct when they feel abandoned by the flock. Even if the flock is in trouble, the bird is usually happier and safer with its own flock. Troubled circumstances pass, and times

come again when old friendships are renewed. The following suggestions do not represent ideal standards of bird care. They are intended for short-term use only.

Sharing Care of Long-lived Species

Sometimes a little vacation, no more than two months each year, can make the difference in a bird's keeping its home. There's nothing wrong with sending the bird to live with its "Aunt" Vera for a few weeks or a few months, especially if the bird is well accustomed to going away and coming back. There may be a big event at home, such as a move to a new house, a marriage, a baby, a divorce, or simply tax time or exam week. Maybe the bird is getting on someone's nerves. Having a temporary place for the bird to stay regularly can do wonders for the parrot/human relationship.

Ideally, the "co-parent" would be someone willing to take over guardianship of the bird in case of your illness or death. This person should know the bird's current habits. Describe the parrot's latest diet, likes, dislikes, and medical history. Make an agreement about the bird's future, covering such issues as whether the bird is to become a breeder. Having this information in writing can help prevent misunderstandings.

At some point the co-parent may decide to get his or her own parrot, especially if the bird is sorely missed when it's away. Decide ahead of time whether this is acceptable or whether there should be a backup co-parent.

Cockatiels are bright, cheerful companions that often adapt easily to a second home.

There are countless types of parrots from which to choose when you decide to adopt a pet. Once you decide on a specific bird to adopt, it's a good idea to research the specific breed thoroughly.

At first, Senegals may be shy in their new home. But they will be as delightfully bossy as any parrot once they settle in.

A close-up of the Umbrella cockatoo's magnificent plumage.

✔ Put the birdcage near human activities so that people can talk to the bird or offer it an occasional "goody." Offer treats whenever possible, even if only as you pass by every day. If you're depressed and stop talking to the bird, it will stop talking to you. The bird will cherish any *"Hello"* or *"Pretty bird"* as though it were a gift.

✔ Be sure the bird has the largest possible cage, especially if there will be no one available to let the bird out and play with it for a few weeks.

✔ Stop chopping vegetables and use frozen mixes for a while. Keep at least a one-month supply of food in the freezer, including both frozen vegetables and the bird's basic pelleted diet. Be sure to leave the original label with the pelleted diet, so that anyone who comes into the house can see what the bird has been eating.

✔ Streamline husbandry. Don't forget to put that stack of newspapers in the bottom of the cage so that top layers can easily be removed. A sheet of clear Plexiglas on the wall behind the cage protects the wall and makes cleaning easy. A plastic drop cloth also works well and is cheaper. Make sure the bird can't reach it!

✔ Combine those important showers (see Exercise and Bathing, page 43) with cage cleaning by sponging the cage after the bird has been sprayed. Especially if the bird is getting little or no time out of the cage, be sure it is treated to a spray bath at least twice weekly. Any cage will tarnish or rust if water is left standing on the surface. Wipe the cage down after it is washed or after the bird is misted. The most common place for rust to appear is the tray. Lightly greasing the tray (try a spray-on, such as Pam, applied in a different room from the bird *only* where the bird *can't* reach it). That procedure will keep poop from sticking and help to prevent rust.

✔ Keep sets of inexpensive plastic shower curtain rings for "toy emergencies." Then, if the bird's toys are totally shot and you can't get to the store to buy toys, you can grab a few shower curtain rings and hang them interspersed with parts from partially demolished toys. These toys won't

Placing the parrot near activity allows family members to give it attention whenever they have a chance, even if those times are brief.

HUSBANDRY

last long, but they can get you through a few days in a pinch. Keep a supply of branches that can be quickly introduced as interesting new perches. Relate perches and toys to the area where the bird poops. Many birds like to be in front of the cage. If they are hanging on the inside front of the cage and there is no perch available, the poop runs either down the bars or onto the floor in front of the cage. Solve this problem with at least one perch that runs from front to back at the place the bird likes to hang. Place toys so that the bird isn't tempted to roost (and poop) on them.

✔ Look for a pet sitter, veterinary technician, or other avian professional to come in occasionally, perhaps once a week, to provide the bird with a little quality time and to do cleaning and feeding chores that you may not be able to do.

✔ Try to set aside at least a few minutes every few days to check in with Paco and comfort him and tell him that you are OK, even if you have to do it by phone. If you can't do that, have someone else do it for you. They can say "Your mom says to be sure to remember her and that she will be home soon and that she loves you and that you are a pretty bird."

Some short cuts can minimize the time spent taking care of the bird without compromising on the quality of the care.

✔ It's possible to make up for inattention by paying extra attention when there's time. If there's a free hour every other Saturday, spend that time with the bird and don't feel guilty about it. It's better to muddle through, even for a year or two, until times are better than to abandon a long-term family member. Don't forget to improve the husbandry when times are easier. As soon as possible after the crisis has passed, try to improve interacting times and diet, and replace perches and toys, even if that must be done gradually.

THE CORRECTIVE ENVIRONMENT

Second-hand parrots come with baggage—emotional baggage, behavioral baggage, sometimes actual baggage—but they seldom come with a good cage. The cage may be a big part of why the bird lost its home in the first place.

The New Cage

An appropriate cage is designed with both the bird and its caretaker in mind. If a cage is difficult to clean, move, or service (changing food, water, toys, and perches), the person responsible for the bird's care can easily lose interest. No one wants to give Polly a cracker if it means dragging out the vacuum and a bucket of soapy water.

Most parrots benefit greatly from moving to a larger cage. Some birds relish the move and have no problem with the change. A shy or insecure bird may prefer to be switched more slowly, or it may do better in a smaller cage until its confidence increases.

A large door makes it easier to get toys, perches, and other accessories into and out of the cage. A large door also makes it easier to remove the bird on a hand. Many parrots do not like to be taken through a door opening, even if it is large. This reluctance might be averted by installing a short perch on the inside of the door. The bird can be lured to the door perch with a treat, and then, as the door opens, the perch (with the bird on it) swings out of the cage. Some birds will cooperate with step-ups more easily from a door or door perch than from a perch inside the cage.

A bottom grate keeps the bird from picking through unsanitary debris that has fallen onto the tray. A removable grate is easier to clean than a stationary one. A deep tray contains mess better than a shallow one. An apron or seed catcher will help to keep stray feathers, food, shredded perches, and dismantled toys inside the cage. Be sure to get more than one set of dishes, so that there will always be clean dishes on hand.

Encouraging independent play can help relieve many behavior problems.

The cage should be made of easy-to-clean metal wire or bars. A baked-on powder-coated finish is easy to sponge clean and resists corrosion. These are often attractive cages that complement decor, rather than eyesores to be pushed farther and farther out of view.

From the parrot's point of view, the cage should be rectangular. Corners provide a sense of security. A round, domed-top cage has no corners, but a square or rectangular cage with an arched top does. Arched-top cages also provide more room inside than play-top cages. If the bird is to spend lots of time in the cage, more room is better. The area inside gives the bird three-dimensional climbing space with perches and toys at diverse heights.

Many people like to let their bird sit on top of its cage. Seeing the bird out of the cage makes the caregiver feel good. A well-designed cage provides most of its climbing and playing opportunities on the inside, however. On top, the bird can only walk back and forth, and there is little space for hanging toys, especially at eye or beak level. Here, vices such as attention-demanding vocalizations, feather-damaging behaviors, or defensiveness related to height can easily develop.

On the Cage or in It?

Barney, a 16-month-old Goffin's cockatoo, was in his second home. Anna, his new guardian, called a parrot behavior consultant immediately, because Barney was noisy. He was her first bird, and the noise he was making was so annoying that she didn't even notice that Barney was also chewing feathers. She had already arranged for a third home.

For most of his life, Barney had been sitting on top of the cage because the people he lived with felt it would give him a greater sense of freedom than being confined to a cage that was obviously too small. Unfortunately, when Barney sat on top of his cage, there really wasn't much to do except preen to the point of wearing out his feathers and beg, loudly, for attention—to the point of wearing out Anna's patience.

CHECKLIST

The Ideal Cage
✔ is rectangular, never round, but may have a high arched top with flat sides.
✔ has an easy-to-clean, durable surface.
✔ is large enough for the parrot to flap without hitting the sides of the cage or the toys inside.
✔ has a large door that joins to the cage with a bar-like space to avoid catching toes (optional).
✔ has horizontal bars on at least two sides to promote climbing.
✔ has a diverse assortment of comfortable, chewable wooden perches.
✔ has a high, removable floor grate.
✔ has more than one set of food and water dishes that can be changed from outside the cage.
✔ has no top tray and a top that is easy for the bird to climb across, from the inside upside down or front side right side up.
✔ has a deep tray and an apron to contain fallen debris.
✔ has wheels so that it can be moved easily for cleaning.

The behavior consultant suggested a larger cage. In the new 24 × 36 × 60 inch (61 × 91.5 × 152.5 cm) arched-top cage, Barney had amazing sideways and upside-down climbing opportunities. No matter where he was, there were branches with bark to chew and climb on, and a variety of toys hung at head level so that his beak was almost automatically deflected to toys instead of to his own feathers.

Inside his cage, Barney prospered. He had a greater variety of exciting things to do than he had when sitting on top of his old cage. He was treated to showers every day, sometimes twice daily, and his diet was improved. Within four months, he had an almost-complete covering of feathers. And he had discontinued the attention-demanding calls that were the real reason Anna had asked for help.

Climbing is a favorite exercise for parrots, especially for indoor birds, who may prefer climbing to flying. Although most parrots are quite capable of climbing vertical bars, they will climb more often if the task is easier. Many older parrots, especially overweight birds, have foot problems. A bird with sore feet will avoid climbing unless climbing is easy. A bird with bad feet may develop beak deformities by overuse of its beak in difficult climbing situations. If there are horizontal bars on at least two sides of the cage, the bird will be more likely to climb and to use the whole cage as a playground.

Bad Cage + Bad Feet = Bad Beak

Sydney, a blue-and-gold macaw, looked very, very old. Many of his feathers didn't lay flat anymore, but curled in all directions. He was thin, and his bare white face was wrinkled, often red. His feet were swollen, and he avoided gripping things with his feet. He wouldn't even hold food in his foot, preferring to eat over the bowl. But his only human was dying, and I really had no choice but to take him, at least temporarily.

Sydney's most curious physical feature was a large round indentation where the notch on the left side of his maxilla (upper beak) should have been. He had a similar grooved indentation on the right side of the mandible (lower beak). I'd never seen that before.

I moved Sydney into my spare room in the round black wrought-iron cage he came with. It was large for a cage of that shape. It had only two horizontal bars, dividing the height of the cage approximately into thirds, to which the upright bars were secured.

Within a day, I knew why his beak was shaped that way. There had been no bowls attached to the sides of the cage. The bird had been fed in crocks on the floor of the cage. Sydney had been sliding up and down the bars, using his beak as a hand, and using his feet as little as possible. It was a long slide from the top of that cage to the bottom. The bars had worn a deep groove into the opposite edges of Sydney's beak, which was always used in exactly the same crossed position as he slid up and down the bars.

I fed Sydney in high bowls near his perch until we could do something about that cage and those feet. His new cage has lots of horizontal bars and a couple of nice, big ladders. Ten years later, Sydney looks like a different bird. His beak looks almost normal, and his feathers are almost perfect. He's sweet and quiet, though he remains emotionally aloof. And he still doesn't like to hold things with his feet.

The Temporary Cage

Sometimes parrots arrive unexpectedly, with little advance notice. What do you do when there's a big bird on the way over and you don't have an extra $500–800 to spend on a big cage?

Mickey Muck, who has observed and participated in dozens, maybe hundreds, of adoptions, suggests that metal, cage-like, break-down dog kennels make wonderful temporary housing. Add bolt-on dishes, chewable branches with bark, and a familiar assortment of toys, and a big bird can make a comfortable home while boarding or relocating. These kennels are not airline-approved, but they do break down easily, so that you can carry or ship them as luggage and your bird can make the flight in an airline-approved kennel. For car travel, the bird can stay in the temporary cage while you are on the road.

These cages are not good for long-term use because they are hard to keep clean and difficult to service. Moreover, birds can learn to escape from them; there aren't enough horizontal bars; and the bar spacing is too wide for many birds. Mickey reports that she has had no problems using them for up to 30 days.

Perches

A parrot needs several chewable perches. If the bird is young, chews feathers, or has not learned to chew, soft or medium-soft branches with bark can help it develop an interest in chewing. Avoid abrasive perches such as those made of concrete, except inside the door or beside the water bowl, where the bird sits only briefly.

Like toys, perches need not cost a lot. Look for branches with bark, preferably birch, willow, or

Placing the new cage next to the old one for a while can help ease the parrot's transition.

Perches that are too smooth or too rough can harm a bird's feet. The best perches have bark with a good texture. The bird's toes should go a little more than halfway around the perch.

citrus. Avoid apple, oak, yew, and cherry. Dried plum, peach, and crabapple branches have especially good texture for helping foot problems.

Match the size of the perches to the size of the bird's feet. If there is even wear on the pads on the underside of the feet, then the bird has been on appropriately sized perches. If the bottoms of the bird's feet show wear in the middle, or palm, then the perches have been mostly too small. If the toenails are extremely short and no longer curve, the perches may have been too large, or the bird may have spent too much time on a grooming perch. Large or abrasive perches can also cause ulcers or smooth spots on the bottom of the "heel," or wrist joint (metacarpal pad).

A bird with balance or coordination problems may need smaller perches with rough or soft bark that can be gripped easily. A bird

You'll probably notice that your parrot will develop a favorite spot to hang out in the cage.

A play area can increase a bird's opportunities to socialize with the family.

with foot problems may need larger perches that it doesn't have to grip at all. Some birds benefit from having a flat piece of lumber or a grate-like wire shelf to sit on. Some birds with limited use of their feet do better with slightly longer-than-usual toenails; others do better with shorter toenails. If foot problems are severe, try padding the perches, perhaps by wrapping them with cotton twine or bias-cut fabric strips. Stiff rope perches may or may not help birds with foot and balance problems. Perches made of limp or unreinforced rope contribute to falling and inactivity. Introduce new perches while the bird is outside the cage.

Situating the Cage

Whether the bird goes to a new cage or stays in its old one, the location of the cage can affect the bird's adjustment. Although the bird needs to be near activity, it also needs to feel secure: Avoid placing the cage in the middle of the room or against a window. A bird located beside a high-traffic doorway may experience fear reactions whenever anyone rushes unexpectedly through the door. An ideal location for most new second-hand parrots is against a wall or in a corner across the room from entrances and heavy traffic areas.

Shelter can be important to a parrot's sense of safety. Many second-hand birds benefit from having the cage partially covered for at least the first few days.

Many parrots are sensitive to height. Some are more comfortable if they are higher, and others prefer to be lower. A parrot that is more comfortable being housed low may prefer to have a barrier, perhaps plants or toys, from behind which it can peek out. Some parrots may defend their higher territory with nips

and calls. Those birds may show a behavior improvement if the cage is lowered.

Play Areas

Giving you bird a separate play area offers more advantages than allowing it to spend time on top of its cage. The bird can be more mobile, joining family members in side-by-side activities anywhere in the home. A low play perch removes the added incentive of height that might cause the bird to be overly territorial. Consider having at least one of the bird's two daily meals in this area. This arrangement encourages cooperative behavior from the bird, because it depends on you to get back and forth between the cage and perch. The parrot may also feel less motivated to defend cage territory if it spends less time there.

The Roost Cage

Fatigue can contribute to many unwanted behaviors. This problem can be addressed with the use of a roost cage. If the bird has been housed in the central area of a large family home, it may have been sleep-deprived for a long time.

A roost cage need not be large or fancy; it is just a safe, quiet place to sleep, away from the bustle of human activity. It can be a travel cage, as this familiar second cage is also good for vacations and other longer outings. Sometimes the bird's old cage can be used as a roost cage. Occasionally the bird's bonds are too strong, however, and it can develop negative behaviors related to wanting to be in the roost cage too much. If the new second-hand parrot does not enter and leave its cage easily, then the regular cage might be rolled to and from a roost area until the bird learns new skills.

Potential Adverse Reactions to the New Cage

Many second-hand birds have been around the block enough times that changing the cage doesn't bother them. Many others have experienced so little change that even a second food bowl or new chewable perches are unsettling. If the parrot has always had the same cage or is very attached to a long-term cage, a new cage must be introduced sensitively.

The bird may sit in the middle of the top perch and refuse to touch the new cage, possibly in reaction to an unfamiliar cage finish or an unfamiliar cage color. This situation can be further complicated if food bowls are made of unfamiliar material or are low, and the bird won't climb down to eat or drink. If the bird is not too upset, it will take its food from human hands. This is a good opportunity for bonding with the bird. The bird can be accommodated by installing food and water bowls up high, within easy reach, for a few days or weeks, and then gradually moving the dishes down to their designated positions in the cage.

Moving to the New Cage

Have the cage already set up with a comfortable assortment of perches and toys, including several large toys toward the front of the cage (but not in front of the door), so that the bird can hide behind them. If the bird arrives early in the day in a box, carrier, or paper bag, it usually can be transferred immediately to the cage. Just put the container inside the cage and open it so that the bird can come out when it is ready. If the bird is in a carrier and arrives late in the day, it might be best to let it spend the night in the carrier.

If the bird comes with a cage, let it stay in the old cage for at least a few days, unless it is totally unsanitary or impossible to clean. Ideally, the second-hand bird should have the opportunity to feel that it has chosen its new cage.

Place the old cage next to the new one. Put food in the dishes in the new cage and open the doors to both cages. Put a couple of favorite or familiar toys in the new cage. If the bird seems reluctant, let another bird demonstrate how much fun the new cage is. Don't shut the door the first time the bird wanders into the new cage, because that could increase its anxiety.

When the bird feels comfortable moving back and forth between the cages, it can start eating in the new cage and spending the day there with the door closed. At this time, food and water dishes can be removed from the old cage. Later, perches and toys can be removed from the old cage and placed in the new one. Once the bird is in the new cage full-time, let the old cage sit there for another day or two before removing it. The whole process could take a few days or a few weeks. (Many of us don't have room for an extra cage in the house. Remember that this arrangement is only temporary, and the room will seem much larger when the old cage is removed!) While the bird is becoming accustomed to the new cage, it should not be left uncaged without supervision. A little extra care to ensure a smooth transition to an appropriate cage can make a huge difference, especially with a sensitive bird. You can't go too slowly when moving to the new cage, and you can't be too careful in selecting features to suit the bird. In the long run, the quality of the bird's life may depend upon the quality of its cage.

BOREDOM: THE GREATEST BATTLE

By the time a parrot is given up for adoption, it may have been neglected for a long time. Some parrots may never have seen a toy; others may have boxes of them, yet may have failed to learn play behaviors.

Why Is a Toy More Than a Plaything?

A toy isn't just something to play with; it has a much more important function in a companion parrot's life. Wild parrots spend their days foraging, fighting, fleeing, defending, building, courting, copulating, raising offspring, destroying, screaming, bathing, flying, and engaging in many other behaviors that are not always welcome in a living room. A companion parrot must learn to use the energy intended for those functions by playing with toys. A toy must fulfill every role, from enemy to nesting site to mate, for a solitary companion parrot. Destructible toys are opportunities for "home improvements." A toy can be something to protect, something to scream at, something to hang from.

A parrot's cage needs plenty of objects that can be destroyed, rearranged, and dismantled.

Bored parrots may entertain themselves in ways that are either self-destructive or detrimental to the bird/human relationship. Behaviors developed by the use of toys keep companion parrots interested, extroverted, and open to change. An ever-changing assortment of safe, challenging toys helps the bird to retain that wild exuberance humans love so dearly.

What Is a Toy?

A second-hand parrot may arrive with only one toy left in the cage, perhaps accompanied by the explanation, "Well, that's the only toy that he didn't chew up!" If the toy was not chewed or dismantled, however, the bird may not have even recognized it as a toy.

A toy isn't necessarily something that costs money. There is no need for a conscientious caregiver to feel guilty about not buying bird toys (they can be quite expensive)! A large

Simple Household Items That Can Be Used to Encourage Playing

✔ Cheap box tape (the kind that isn't too sticky) wrapped around a chunk of cotton rope (not more than 1.5 inches [3.8 cm] long) or around a strip of denim cut on the bias like shoestring tips.

✔ Wooden spoons.

✔ Pompoms made from newspaper (or other plain, not shiny, paper).

✔ Cardboard tubes—pieces of rolls from (untreated) paper towels. Whole rolls of toilet paper work well for feather pluckers.

✔ Junk mail (dull paper) either on a skewer made for birds or woven in the cage bars.

✔ Old jeans or cotton fabric cut into strips (on the bias so that threads aren't long) and tied to the cage bars or to other toys.

✔ Old telephone books.

✔ Popsicle sticks, plastic straws, paper cups, or paper plates. Punch holes in the cups and plates and weave straws and popsicle sticks through them.

✔ Some plastic toys made for children (make sure toes and feet can't get caught in them).

✔ Chunks of scrap (untreated) lumber. Raid the local lumber store's trash bins (with permission, of course). If you are cutting your own, make the pieces angled (easier to chew) instead of square.

Parrots like toys with parts that move and parts that can be destroyed or dismantled. A toy can be a simple thing. Just think, would a child rather play with a designer doll in designer clothes or a carton of crayons and a refrigerator box? Parrots and children operate on much the same frequency. A huge box offers more intellectual freedom, more possibilities, more types of rewards than an expensive doll. For a parrot, destroying something supplies the kind of satisfaction it might get perfecting a nesting site, discovering a wonderful food source, or driving off a rival. A cardboard box can supply as much satisfaction as a $60 toy. (Be sure the box is clean and new and that it has never had food in it.)

The best parrot toy is safe, and that can be a tall order. For example, many toys come with string, rope, or fabric parts that a parrot can become entangled in, especially macaws, which like to snuggle in and around their toys (a comfort behavior). No matter how safe you think a toy is, take it for a "test drive" by watching the way the bird plays with it. Are there places where toes get caught or small parts that could be swallowed? If so, remove the toy immediately.

The best toys stimulate the bird's curiosity and inspire interaction. Many common household items make safe, inexpensive toys, and they may be less scary to a parrot who has had little exposure to real parrot toys.

Learning What to Do with Toys

A well-adjusted companion parrot knows what to do with a toy: bop it, bite it, dismantle it, chew the pieces to splinters. A bird that

macaw can destroy $100 worth of toys in a week if given the chance. If the toy budget seems high, take a look at the cost of a saw, a drill, and a two-by-four. A few tools can save hundreds of dollars and provide countless hours of happy enterprise for a parrot.

hasn't seen a new toy in years may be terrified, however. If the bird is actively afraid of toys, humans must first demonstrate that the toy won't hurt anybody. Parrots learn by watching comrades, human and avian, and by copying their behavior. Humans may first have to wear, bop, bite, or dismantle a toy in the bird's presence before the bird will even touch it. Wearing toys is especially effective (and becoming to just the right partner). If the bird likes you or likes to watch you, even if it pretends not to, your delighted response to the toy can motivate the bird to copy your behavior.

Let the parrot see that the object is not dangerous by leaving it nearby on a table or shelf where it can be seen from the cage. Once the bird is comfortable with the object at a distance, move it closer to the cage. Eventually, hang it from the outside of the cage before putting it inside. Because it is often frightening to a bird to witness items being placed inside the cage, take the bird out of the room before installing toys or moving them closer to the cage.

Once Beaker no longer thinks the toy will attack her, it's time to convince Beaker to attack the toy. A game of "keep away" will often accomplish this.

Some birds can be tricked into accepting new toys. If the bird likes to chew paper and can first be induced to chew a paper towel tied to a cage bar or perch, then it might be motivated to chew a paper towel off a toy. Once the toy is revealed, the bird might be able to figure out what to do with it. If the bird has first been desensitized to the look of the paper towel "bows," then every toy that comes with a paper towel tied around it will look familiar. The bow becomes a signal that the item is not dangerous.

Keep Away

The favorite person can play this game alone with the bird, but it is more effective with additional participants. Body language is important. Begin by placing the bird on a perch or simply opening the cage door. Stand in front of the bird with the toy in hand.

Briefly offer the toy, just until the bird starts to back away.

Immediately withdraw the offer and focus full attention on the toy.

Do not look at the bird. Turn sideways. Concentrate on playing with the toy. Make lots of loud, happy noises. Pick at the toy, shake it and rub it against your face. Continue talking about how wonderful it is to have the toy.

Periodically offer the toy to the bird again. If the bird continues to show wariness, whisk the toy away, and state that you never intended to share it anyway. If there is another person (especially a child) or bird or even a willing dog or cat around, share the toy with them, but not with the bird. Eventually the bird will touch the toy with its beak. Be sure the bird is ready to play before allowing it to have the toy. Most birds will readily interact with the toy after a few minutes of "keep away," but some may require additional sessions.

If the bird is a good eater, sometimes merely putting a toy on top of food in the bowl will stimulate it to pick up the toy and throw it to the cage bottom or even out of the cage. Lavish praise on the bird for even touching the toy. It's

Some birds take advantage of any opportunity to play and appreciate a variety of toys.

Paper, wood blocks, leather strips, and pieces of rope and cloth make excellent, inexpensive toys for birds to destroy. The wood can be dyed with food coloring.

Flapping exercises can be encouraged by rolling, or raising and lowering the bird on a hand-held perch.

Parrots really enjoy being part of the family.

Unsupervised interactions between children and parrots can be harmful to both. With appropriate precautions, children and parrots can get along very well.

For some birds, spending time on top of the cage can increase behavior problems due to boredom or defending territory.

Many birds will show their interest in taking a bath by splashing in their water dish.

The average kitchen holds many hazards for the pet bird. Be sure to use bird-safe cookware, such as this enamel-coated pan.

What About Bob?

"I want an African grey!"

Almost anyone who meets Bob says that. People said it when he was a baby, and they say it now, but it wasn't always that way. From the beginning, every effort was made to give Bob the best care. He had a warm, loving home, great cage, modern diet, and mountains of toys. He responded by revealing extreme intelligence. He was playful, talkative, and capable of letting his desires be known.

Bob loved to invent and play games, with the reward being a human's reaction. Unfortunately, he learned inappropriate games. His nickname became "the bird that bites *really* hard." He delighted in delivering an ear-shattering screech directly into a human ear. The more he played these games, the less humans wanted to play with him. He experimented with being even more demanding and obnoxious and found he could still get reactions. But as there were fewer people to interact with, he became increasingly insecure.

By the age of nine, the parrot that was once a premium hand-fed was featherless. Bob's human had gladly accommodated his every demand but had failed to fill his need for behavioral guidance. Overwhelmed, Bob's guardian decided to find him a new home.

Bob's fortunes would reverse again. By the time he was 11, even experienced parrot lovers often said that Bob was the nicest parrot they'd ever seen. He was beautiful, sweet, interactive. At 13, he steps carefully onto a child's arm and offers anyone who passes his neck to be scratched. He enjoys adding his opinion to nearby conversations. Bob has an amazing number of admirers who often stop by to see him. Many have asked to take him home, even though they know he's a family pet. Scores of people who wanted a bird have walked away empty-handed because after they'd met Bob, no other bird would do!

Although Bob's changes seem magical, no magic was involved. Bob entered a flock whose members were rewarded for peaceful, quiet, cooperative, appropriate behavior. He was reinforced only for those behaviors. The old behaviors disappeared. Within months, he acted like the other birds, with this exception: Bob not only learned the other birds' behaviors, but performed them better, more successfully, than the other birds!

easy to gain acceptance of paper towels with wadded-up paper towels or paper towels tied in knots on top of dry food or stuck between cage bars. Many parrots, especially cockatoos, seem to relish throwing things out of the cage or putting them into their water bowls. Many birds will first touch a toy if it is floating in the water bowl. Be sure the bird doesn't avoid eating and drinking if these techniques are used. Some very sensitive birds may avoid the bowls entirely.

Another trick is to place easy-to-chew toys in annoying places. Weave strips of paper or untreated leather in and out of cage bars where the bird likes to look out. Stick a paper pompom at eye level where the bird usually stands. Put a cardboard tube on a favorite perch so that the bird has to chew it off in order to walk all the way across the perch. Put toys in food dishes when the food is gone. Once the bird tolerates the introduction of toys, try to offer at least two new (or reintroduced) toys at one time, in different parts of the cage (but not in a way that makes the bird feel surrounded). In this way, the bird can experience a sense of control through the process of deciding which toy to unwrap, play with, bop, or dismantle first.

Many old toys can be sterilized by running them through the dishwasher. This is also a good way to sterilize small cages, grates, and cage parts.

Until the bird learns that play is its own reward, reinforce play by giving rewards when the bird shows interest in toys, even if it's accidental. Exciting verbal rewards will sometimes cause the bird to be more excited about the toy. As with vocalizations, look for any excuse to reward the bird, to help it develop independent play behaviors. As the bird learns to play, the behavior becomes self-rewarding and often replaces attention-demanding behavior.

Exercise and Bathing

Wild parrots have to be strong enough to fulfill every function necessary to survive in the wild in spite of adversities of weather, interference from humans, and an ever-changing environment. A healthy companion parrot inherits a tremendously energetic metabolism from its wild ancestors. Unless that energy is used, the bird will develop behaviors that are not appropriate indoors. Exercise and bathing help the parrot to use its energy in ways that are not destructive to itself, the environment, or the human/bird relationship.

Playing

A companion parrot's exercise opportunities are usually limited to holding on to something—usually the cage, perch, etc.—and flapping; swinging from a hanging toy and flapping; climbing; and chewing. Most birds love (bird-safe) bells; many birds love swings. Provide as many opportunities for exercise as possible.

Flapping

Flapping, by stimulating the bird's metabolism, can alleviate many behavioral issues. Flapping can be encouraged by raising and lowering the bird on a hand or on a hand-held perch or ladder, or by rolling the hand, perch, or ladder on which the bird is sitting. A normal, healthy bird should be encouraged to flap a couple of times a day in addition to the exercise it gets on its own.

When beginning an exercise program with an older bird, be sure to get a veterinary checkup first. The program might complicate health issues, especially heart disease.

Bathing

Showers are similar to exercise in terms of the way the bird's metabolism is stimulated, challenged, and subsequently relaxed. In dry climates, a companion parrot should be very wet at least several times weekly. If the bird has not been bathed with regularity, it may be noisy, high-strung, fearful, nippy, or given to feather-damaging behaviors. Unfortunately, a bird may resist bathing. Worse still, if it has been punished with a spray bottle, it may be afraid of being sprayed.

top left: A game of "keep away" will often get a reluctant bird interested in toys. First find some willing participants to play with the toy in front of the bird.

top right: Then show the toy to the bird briefly before playing with it again. Make sure the attention is on the toy and not the bird.

right: The Goddess Athena (left) had chewed off most of her feathers, yet she attracted her handsome mate Caesar (right), who preferred her to a younger hen in perfect feather. (Umbrella cockatoos)

A bird enjoying a bath will get sillier as it gets wetter. It may exhibit the same or an even more enthusiastic response to being blown dry with a hair dryer. (Yellow-headed Amazon)

Life in the wild is hard for parrots, and wild parrots have to be able to do everything they do to survive even when it's raining. They are genetically determined not only to tolerate rainfall, but to need it. It's part of a parrot's nature to enjoy showers, as seen when they stretch their wings, fan their tails, and puff out their feathers apparently trying to catch every precious raindrop.

It's also part of a parrot's nature to fear anything unfamiliar and to hold a grudge. This can make giving a shower to a poorly socialized parrot a real challenge. Many have

been squirted for "bad" behavior and others have never been sprayed at all. While a parrot might really appreciate a bath, it might also be afraid of anything that sprays water. Many birds have come to associate water hitting them with something that sprays water. This can mean that the instant they feel water hit them they are no longer in the mood for a shower.

The easiest way to help a parrot overcome this fear of showers is to borrow a bird that likes showers. Standing so that the spray bottle is hidden from the frightened

bird, spray the willing bird. Give verbal praise and occasionally send a spray of water toward the scared bird. Eventually, the nervous one will catch on. Help things along by turning the thermostat up or the air conditioner off. A hot bird loves a cool shower.

If there is no other bird to model appropriate behavior, the process is a little slower, but not impossible. The biggest challenge is getting the bird into the mood. This is a matter of figuring out the bird's preferences. Again, a warmer-than-usual room is a good place to start. Often, running a vacuum cleaner or dishwasher will help the bird get in the mood. If the bird starts dunking his head in his water dish, exploit this opportunity for him to learn to enjoy showers by also misting him.

Mist is almost always tolerated better than spray with droplets. Seeing the droplets fly through the air can be scary to many birds. Mist is also more efficient in wetting the bird, as droplets have greater surface tension and hold together better when they hit the bird, often rolling off the bird's feathers rather than moistening the feathers as mist would do.

Many birds will be inspired to bathe at the sound of a vacuum cleaner.

Experiment with different times of day, different water temperatures, and different locations. Try misting the bird slightly and then running the vacuum or misting the plants before going back to finish the bird's shower. Let the bird sit in the bathroom while a human takes a shower. Play a recording of a thunderstorm while misting the parrot.

Many parrots are afraid of anything that sprays water. Experiment with different-looking spray bottles and other devices to deliver the water. A bird might be afraid of a large red bottle but not a small yellow one. A bird that can't tolerate a spray bottle might appreciate a fine mist attachment on the hose.

Some parrots are attracted to the kitchen sink by watching their favorite humans working and cleaning in the kitchen. Some of these birds like to dunk their heads under the regular faucet, some prefer to be sprayed with the sprayer attachment from the sink. Many parrots enjoy having their cages taken outdoors during a light rainfall or when a lawn sprinkler might occasionally reach the cage or a part of the cage.

Reluctant birds can sometimes be enticed to bathe in a warm room in a heavy, clear, shallow dish such as a glass pie pan. Some birds like the water cool, some like it warm. Almost all birds like to play with ice cubes or other floating objects, an activity that can stimulate bathing.

Some parrots, especially smaller parrots, like "leaf bathing." This is accomplished when they

Some birds prefer to bathe in a shallow dish.

rub themselves into wet objects. Very small parrots, such as budgies, parrotlets, and lovebirds, might leaf bathe in lettuce or other greens. Larger birds, such as Sally Blanchard's monkey-like caique, might be determined to rub their bodies into wet human hair. Spraying the bird while it is in the cage can provide opportunities to leaf bathe in familiar toys with rope or fabric parts. These toys can then be removed and run through the dishwasher before being returned dry to the bird's cage.

Coaxing a shy, nervous parrot to recover a natural love of water may require sensitive persistence. That persistence sooner or later can bring big payoffs. Improvements in all aspects of the bird's behavior can be almost immediately observed with just a few baths. Frequent drenching showers can make a difference in nipping, biting, and unwanted screaming and feather-damaging behaviors in a matter of hours.

SPECIALIZED CARE IN THE NEW HOME

Stress endangers a bird's ability to stay healthy, and the new bird generally suffers the most stress, perhaps because it was receiving poor care or was traumatized by having to leave a good home.

For those who already have a bird, the idea of bringing in another one can be scary. Chances are, the new bird hasn't had the best care, and there's a possibility that it might be hiding one or more communicable illnesses.

Monitoring the Bird's Health

Assuming the care of a parrot is easier if the bird is healthy and comes with a complete medical history. Start with a veterinarian you trust. Try to find a board-certified avian veterinarian or a veterinarian who is well known for expertise in avian medicine, rather than one who treats mostly dogs and cats. Comparing blood work done at this time with future or past tests can reveal change or stability in the bird's health.

Even birds that look great may be harboring an illness. A trip to the avian veterinarian and quarantine procedures will reduce the risk of spreading disease to other birds in the home.

While waiting for those tests to come back, or until you can get to the veterinarian, monitor the bird's health by weighing it every few days before it eats for the first time that day. Small weight fluctuations such as 5 or 10 grams are not unusual. For a generally thin bird with a prominent breastbone, weighing can show whether the bird is losing additional weight, a fact that would cause concern. With an obese bird with fat feet, fat toes, flabby breast tissue, and a fat pad under the tail, it might be good to see stable or slightly declining (less than 5 percent per day) weight.

A clean bill of health from the veterinarian can help the bird's new caretaker breathe easier. Assuming that this means the bird is disease-free, however, can be dangerous. There are illnesses that cannot be detected with tests. Even illnesses that can be detected sometimes escape detection. In many cases, the bird must be sick to the point of compromised organ function for the illness to show up in lab work. Birds thought to carry serious communicable diseases such as PBFD (Psittacine Beak and

Fatty Liver Disease

Out of love and good intentions, many people feed their birds whatever the birds want to eat. When the birds realize what pushovers their humans are, they begin demanding a sunflower seed and French fry diet. As a result, many second-hand parrots are fat.

One of the problems obese birds face is fatty liver degeneration. Excess fat in the diet (or lack of certain fatty acids) can result in fat buildup in the liver, a condition that decreases liver function. This disease can be fatal to the bird, but if it is diagnosed early, sometimes diet change can allow the liver to mend. Excessive beak growth can indicate liver disease. Sometimes toenails are also affected. It may take a year or more for beak and toenail growth to return to normal after correction of the diet.

If the veterinarian feels the bird is fat, try to change its diet immediately. If the bird doesn't see any sunflower seeds or French fries around, it won't be as likely to hold out for those items. Offer a variety of healthful snacks. If the bird is Quaker-sized or larger, it may hold out for more than a day before trying anything new. (Small birds, even fat ones, can starve if they go more than a day without food.) If the bird is rejecting new, healthful items, contact your behavior consultant or veterinarian. After all, you want to avoid a starvation situation.

Try warm, soft food that you can eat in front of the bird, including sweet potatoes, bananas, and mangoes. If the bird was hand-fed, offer it some hand-feeding formula, even if the bird is definitely not a baby. If the bird insists on seed, give it small, sprouted seeds like millet, canary grass, and buckwheat.

Although fatty liver disease is extremely serious and life-threatening, it can be survivable if caught in time. Change to a proper diet is considered the primary correction factor; however, often nutritional supplements and medications are also needed. Some holistic therapies have been reported amazingly effective.

Feather Disease) or PDD (Proventricular Dilatation Disease) should never be kept in the same house with healthy birds. Birds with diseases such as Polyomavirus or Pox virus must be kept away from other birds until the viruses run their course, at which time they can safely be around other birds again.

Quarantine

The veterinarian's workup is the first step to protecting established birds. Quarantine is the next. In most homes, a true quarantine is impossible. That would require the new bird to be located in a room that did not share the same air supply as the rest of the house. It would also require the caregiver to shower and change clothes and shoes whenever leaving the quarantine area. That type of isolation does little to make the new bird feel secure in its new home.

Keep the new bird as separate as possible from resident birds without driving everyone crazy. If the birds can't be kept in separate rooms, keep them as far apart as possible.

In general, diseases are not highly contagious between adult companion parrots. Simple hygiene is usually sufficient to prevent the spread of disease in a group of separately housed individuals. Most communicable avian diseases are spread by fecal material and feather dander. Wash hands after handling, feeding, or cleaning up. Keep clean papers in the cage bottom, even changing them twice daily if possible. Wash dishes in the dishwasher after every feeding (don't forget the water dishes!), or soak them in disinfectant and rinse well. Keep plenty of extra dishes. Some people use different-colored dishes for the new bird. When tending the birds, visit the new bird's cage last.

Consult with the veterinarian about how long quarantine should last. If the bird appears healthy, a month may be adequate. A bird of questionable health may require as long as six months. Sixty days is average.

Chronic Health Problems

Although a very young parrot may come with a hidden acute disease, ill health in an older parrot is more likely to be a chronic or long-term problem related to inadequate physical stimulation, poor lighting, poor nutrition, or poor hygiene. The most common chronic health problems are often related to poor diet, but even infectious diseases are more easily acquired by malnourished birds.

Birds that have lived on seeds exclusively may be suffering from vitamin A deficiency. Long-term lack of vitamin A affects the skin and mucous membranes. There may be feather cysts, badly shaped or curled feathers growing from unhealthy feather follicles (abnormalities that may also appear with PBFD or any of several other factors). Signs of vitamin A deficiency can sometimes be seen inside the bird's mouth. If the

little points lining the opening at the back of the throat (choanal papillae) are sharp and well defined, the bird is more likely to be healthy and not suffering from vitamin A deficiency.

Any parrots, but especially African parrots, may have poor grip or clenched or spasmodic feet, associated with calcium deficiency, as well as a tendency to break bones easily. The bird's metabolism, including effective use of calcium, vitamin A, vitamin D, and other nutrients, is influenced by the amount and quality of the lighting the bird experiences. Studies done by Hagan Laboratories in Canada have demonstrated that parrots do best in regular fluorescent lighting, rather than incandescent lighting or full-spectrum fluorescent lighting.

A parrot living in semidarkness becomes emotionally, and ultimately physically, depressed. Its metabolism gradually slows down, and inadequate processing of nutrients, including calcium, results. In a breeding setting, that means fewer eggs. For a companion, it means slower molts, resulting in increasingly poor feather condition. Especially if the bird has been kept in a dark interior room, gradually increase levels of good lighting as soon as it is comfortable in the new home.

Balanced Nutrition

Most parrots love to eat, and yummy treats can be an open door to friendship with a second-hand parrot. Balanced nutrition is another matter. Feeding a parrot can be as difficult as feeding a child. Send a kid to school with a healthy sandwich, carrots, an apple, and a cookie, and you have provided a potentially balanced diet. Unfortunately, the child often eats the cookie and trades the rest for a

Portia at age 20 loves to display when allowed height. (Yellow-naped Amazon)

Mmmm, Yummm

I'd heard other breeders talking about feeding live mealworms to their parent birds. They said that parrots in the wild eat insects when there is an opportunity. So when I happened upon some giant mealworms that were specially bred for pet consumption, I offered them to my birds.

Some of the birds just backed away from the dish, their glances bouncing back and forth between me and the worm. Others actually screamed and clung to the back of the cage in terror. It was clear I had no takers.

Not wanting the worms to go to waste, my daughter and I gathered them up and fed them to our turtles, which happened to be in full view of the parrots. We were laughing and pointing as the turtles were chasing and chomping.

Then we realized the parrots were saying "Want some!" So we went around again, putting mealworms into the parrots' dishes. This time, almost every parrot tried them. Some were even fighting over them.

If this works with mealworms, imagine what might happen with food that doesn't move!

cupcake and some pudding. Likewise, a parrot might eat what it likes and throw the rest to the dog or the baby crawling on the floor.

Poor nutrition has serious, long-term consequences for a parrot. An older bird might take five years or more to recover from malnutrition, in spite of being offered a perfectly

Most parrots, even this Senegal, will try to control what people feed it and may throw temper tantrums to get their favorite foods.

Pionus, Amazons, Senegals, and budgerigars often have problems with obesity. Limiting access to high-calorie fatty foods can help prevent fatty liver disease.

nutritious diet. Some consequences of malnutrition are so severe that the bird might never recover fully. Moreover, all that might have occurred in spite of honorable efforts by everyone caring for the bird.

Although avian nutritional research has been going on for years, we still don't know the perfect diet, and with the vast number of avian species, we may never find a formula that is right for all parrots. The best source of diet

Some smaller birds, such as this plum-headed parakeet, will not switch over to a pelleted diet. Adding fresh sprouted seed to their diet can improve their nutrition.

Pellets: To Feed or Not to Feed

Starting from scratch and providing a consistently complete parrot diet is not easy. Pellets greatly simplify the process. Most busy people cannot chop vegetables and cook for their parrot companion every day. Pellets fill in where human energy leaves off, providing the micronutrients important to the bird's health. They are much less messy than seed.

Read the label before selecting a pellet, especially if you wish to avoid artificial colors and flavors. Further, don't be afraid to taste the food. If it tastes bitter to you, it'll be hard to get the bird to eat it. Some pellet companies use chemical odor enhancers on the pellets to give them a fruity smell, which may be pleasant or annoying to the owner.

information is, therefore, aviculturists with years of successful experience.

Vegetables should make up the largest part of the diet. Colorful fruits and vegetables such as sweet potatoes, beets, carrots, squash, mangoes, papaya, and green peas are more nutritious than corn, green grapes, or apples. Some birds eat seed in the wild, but most do not thrive on seed in captivity. Lories, more intolerant of seed than other birds, typically need more fruits and protein than other parrots.

Because parrots control what they actually put into their beaks, figuring out how to feed is as important as figuring out what to feed, in most cases.

Most second-hand birds need at least a diet revision, and many need a complete diet overhaul. The first step is human cooperation. Dad's best efforts to provide a perfect diet will be foiled if Mom is giving Polly peanuts and potato chips on the side. Cooperation also simplifies the process of introducing new foods. Parrots copy not only what they hear, but also what they see. If someone is happily munching a carrot, the parrot probably will want a bite. At least the bird will start to show interest and curiosity. If the person eating the carrot is praised and the carrot is passed around to other excited members of the household (even if those members are dogs, cats, or other birds), the bird will likely want to join in.

Dietary habits can be extremely resistant to change. A "seed junkie" second-hand parrot cannot be forced to eat vegetables even if it is given nothing else to eat. It may not realize that these strange, scary things (the vegetables) are actually food. Just imagine offering a hamburger-eating teenager eels or octopus. It's helpful to establish a feeding routine, intro-

duce some sneaky tricks at the same time, and, above all, be patient!

Start by giving vegetables or soft food every morning. Provide seed in the evening and take the seed out of the cage before bedtime. Use a seed mix with mostly small seeds and, for now, no high-fat seeds such as sunflower or safflower. Canary seed, buckwheat, and millet provide more protein than safflower seed.

Try sprinkling a few (a countable number) small seeds on the vegetables. Puree some vegetables and mix them with eggs and seed. Cook this mixture in the microwave to make a bird "omelet" that can be frozen in portion-sized packages. Be careful not to offer this mixture directly from the microwave. The same thing can be done with cornbread mix. Gradually increase the size of the vegetable pieces and decrease the amount of seed.

Continue offering healthy choices, no matter how long it takes, even if it takes a year! Optimize nutrition from the seed mix by making sure the seed is fresh. Some bulk seed, such as seed from mills, may be cleaner and fresher than prepackaged types. Try coating the seed with mashed sweet potatoes or mangoes. Soak the seed in water overnight to bring it back to life. Better yet, sprout the seed by keeping it rinsed and damp (not submerged!) in a paper towel or tea towel overnight. Fresh seed sprouts in a few days. It's best served while it still looks like a seed rather than a bean sprout.

Eventually, with veterinarian approval, most companion parrots should be switched to pellets. This process may be a battle of wills. If the bird has been on an all-seed diet, Paul Welch, D.V.M., of Tulsa reminds us to offer some seed, even if the seed is available for only 15 minutes twice daily, to avoid a starvation risk. Dr.

Wing feathers should be trimmed carefully. A more restrictive trim is used on very good fliers.

Welch also suggests pellets and fruits as between-meal snacks. Once the bird has begun to eat soft food, start to sprinkle a few pellets in with the seed or on the soft food. Don't be surprised if the pellets that are mixed in with seed are ignored or tossed. Once the bird is readily consuming pellets, alternate evening meals—one day seed, the next day pellets— gradually phasing out the seed.

Some parrots, such as Australian cockatoos, grass parakeets, budgerigars, and cockatiels, may totally resist being switched to pellets. Be careful not to starve the bird. Continue offering vegetables and sprouted seed.

Corrective Grooming

A second-hand bird may not have been groomed in a long time. Grooming of wing feathers, toenails, and, if necessary, the beak should be done, especially the first time, by an experienced professional groomer, aviculturist, or veterinarian. Low-stress grooming can be scary the first time; however, wing trims and conditioning to tolerate grooming are impor-

tant parts of being a responsible parrot provider. Wing trims can be a life-or-death issue for a companion parrot. Ideally, a companion parrot's wings are trimmed in the most noninvasive configuration necessary to prevent indoor flight. Wings are trimmed symmetrically so that the bird has balance and the process of flapping remains pleasurable. Parrots have an easier time growing wing feathers if wings are never trimmed shorter than the layer of feathers (coverts) that protects the bases of the long wing feathers (primary flight feathers) as they grow in. Feathers should never be trimmed so short that the bird cannot glide into a landing. That can be very important to young birds, fearful birds, clumsy birds, or birds with bad feet.

Trim any toenail that lifts the end of the toe off a flat surface.

Feather picking can be a sign of a chronic health problem, but often there are many other stressors involved as well.

This grey's wings are trimmed for a moderately strong bird. For young or out-of-shape birds, take only a little off the first three or four feathers. For stronger birds, these feathers can be clipped back to the coverts. The coverts (feathers covering the base of the primaries) and secondary feathers (long feathers closest to and pointing toward the body) should never be cut.

Parrots need to chew to keep their beaks in good condition. If allowed to, they will often pick inappropriate objects to satisfy this need.

The new bird may become interested in being held when it sees another bird enjoying the interaction.

A second-hand bird may have suffered a reaction to a wing trim that rendered it unable to grow wing feathers or may, at some time, have chewed wing feathers. An examination by an avian veterinarian may discover feather cysts, which may require surgery. If a feather cyst has been present for a while, it may be painful, and may have been one of the reasons the bird lost its home. Sometimes a follicle can be damaged to the extent that it heals over and no longer produces feathers. Wings may require veterinary intervention as a part of the rehabilitation process. Especially if the bird is clumsy or has leg, foot, or gripping problems, don't let anybody trim the bird's wings shorter than the coverts.

Overgrown nails may be needle sharp, even curved into circles. If the bird is known to be

shy, toenails should be merely blunted slightly and brought into manageable length so that they will not become trapped in things. Enough toenail should remain to help the bird grip the unfamiliar perches in the new environment. Perches should have natural bark that ranges from soft to medium hard and should be small enough for the bird to grip tightly. Larger perches can be added later, but if the bird is skittish, it could get hurt falling from large, hard perches.

Parrots with severe calcium deficiency or a liver abnormality may have thin blood that does not clot properly. Groom the toenails of second-hand birds with great care and always with a good coagulant, such as a styptic powder or pencil. Just in case there's an emergency, groom

Hazards in the Home

A companion parrot can be injured or killed in household accidents. The majority of these accidents are associated with access, usually by flying, to

✔ standing water in the tub, toilet, sink, hot tub, or aquarium

✔ frying pans, cooking stoves, and open fireplaces

✔ entanglement trauma: loose strings in toys and towels and afghans

✔ doors and windows (open or closed)

✔ larger pets

✔ ceiling fans, electrical cords, swinging doors, and recliners

✔ inappropriate bar spacing or poorly designed caging

✔ toxic plants

✔ fumes from second-hand smoke

✔ almost any burning plastic, including polytetrafluorethylene (Teflon)

✔ household pesticides, medications, room deodorants, and scented candles

✔ dietary toxins, including alcohol, avocado, chocolate, and moldy foods

second-hand parrots during bird-hospital hours. Better yet, let the veterinarian groom the new bird until more is known about its health. Some birds will eventually tolerate or enjoy grooming by the primary caretaker. If it makes you nervous and upset to groom the bird, however, and if it makes the bird nervous and upset, then have a professional groomer or veterinarian do it. Many cities now have experienced behavior consultants or in-home groomers who can come to your home for routine grooming.

Beaks, too, may have grown malformed and may require professional grooming, as well as habitat modification, to get into shape again (see Bad Cage + Bad Feet = Bad Beak, page 31). Overgrown beaks may be the result of poor diet or, in budgies, a common parasite called scaly face, a tiny mite that can be easily eradicated by an avian veterinarian. Beaks that have been damagedmay need regular trimming to remain in usable configurations. A bird with beak irregularity should come with instructions if the beak or the wings routinely require exceptional or unusual maintenance.

Contaminated Feathers

A bird occasionally comes with horribly contaminated feathers. Almost always, a few showers with plain water will resolve this problem, but occasionally, plain water won't do. This may be a bird that got into cosmetics or petroleum products, a bird that lived with serious tobacco smokers, or a bird that is biting off feathers with lipstick on them. As with wild birds contaminated by oil spills, a little soap may be necessary.

Nicotine toxicity has been shown to contribute to extreme self-mutilation. The nicotine may be absorbed through the inhalation of smoke or from a smoker's fingers, irritating the bird's skin and legs. In one case, a bird chewed its toe off in the veterinarian's waiting room. Mattie Sue ultimately had to shampoo that bird.

Shampooing is a rare but beneficial technique for birds with obvious adverse reactions to contaminated feathers. This procedure isn't for removing a little dried food on the face, but for dealing with something like brown tobacco-smoke residue, which can contribute to self-mutilation. Gentle shampooing may be needed if a bird is chewing contaminated feathers.

Teflon Story

I did an in-home consultation for Charley, a new/used cockatoo, the family's first bird. He had a reputation as a biter, a maverick, a bird that would never be tame. He had lived for seven years in a 2-foot (61 cm) diameter domed cage.

Imagine the tearful scene when we discovered immediately that Charley was very, very tame and starved to be touched. We spent almost the entire two hours cuddling and petting and weeping over this darling bird, which had been denied touch for seven long years.

Later during the consultation, I noted that there was Teflon cookware much in evidence.

"Of course, you'll want to replace your cookware," I suggested.

They laughed, "For a bird? We have no intention of replacing our cookware for a bird!"

No amount of my earnest stories was enough to change their minds.

Fortunately, our meeting was nearly ended. I didn't hear from them for over a year. Then a newspaper story reported that Charley had saved their grandson's life by calling his name as he slept near a Teflon pan on fire. The young man survived that accident, but the bird did not.

Fumes from overheated polytetrafluoroethylene (the material used in Teflon and almost all other nonstick cookware) can kill a parrot during a single brief accident. This situation most commonly occurs when a pan is cooked dry. If you have a parrot, you owe it to your bird and to yourself to find safer cookware. Don't forget that polytetrafluoroethylene can be on irons, space heaters, and bread-baking machines. Accidents involving those products can also be fatal for the bird. Fumes from many other burning plastics can also be fatal to birds.

Wildlife rehabilitators use dishwashing soap, which is considered safe, as is very mild shampoo. Don't use heavy detergents and especially, do not use Woolite (a product formulated to dissolve protein) on the bird's feathers. Because feathers are made of protein, Woolite would damage them.

Contamination may be localized. Start by nestling the bird in a large towel. Use clean, fresh water in a spray bottle at very close range (2–3 inches or 5–7.5 cm) to moisten an area of a few square inches, perhaps the middle of the back, a common site for oil damage from the touch of human hands. Applying a few drops of soap to your fingertips, rub it a bit between your thumb and fingers. Apply the soap to the moist feathers by rubbing those few wet feathers between your thumb and fingers, with a motion that gently pulls the feather filaments in the direction of their growth. Don't scrub the feathers against the direction of growth.

Next, covering the bird's head and isolating the affected area with the towel, spray the soapy area with water, rub the shampoo out of the feathers, and then spray again until the shampoo is thoroughly rinsed. If the bird is properly cradled in the towel, all the rinse water is absorbed by the towel, rather than possibly going into the bird's eyes or mouth. You may have to use more than one towel. Rest, observe the bird's response, and then repeat on other affected areas.

ACCLIMATION

The first few months in the home are an opportunity to stimulate and reinforce new behaviors you'd like to see again. Every effort should be made to convince the bird that it has moved to paradise. Many, possibly most, birds respond positively and immediately to these efforts. Some birds do not.

Occasional Adverse Reactions

A wild bird is in danger of dying when separated from its flock. Add to that the stress of separation from a mate. Even if both the "mate" and the "flock" were humans who did a lousy job, the bird may react to loss of those important relationships. A bird reacting to the stress of change may damage feathers or call incessantly. It's important to respond to distress calls at this time. Do your best to alleviate any discomfort the bird may be experiencing.

A little shyness or fearfulness can be expected, because most parrots are cautious when things change. A bird may avoid coming out of the cage or even avoid moving around inside the cage. It may increase reliance on the fight-or-flight response (the instinct to bite or fly away when confronted).

Some birds may need more time to acclimate than others. Move forward with interactions only once the bird feels comfortable at the current level. (Buffon's macaw)

This is a good time to keep out of harm's way. Avoid the development of a biting habit by giving the bird no opportunity to bite. Give the bird lots of space, and spend lots of time in nonthreatening positions (on the floor or lying down or with your back to the bird) talking to the bird.

Interacting Without Touching

Some companion birds enjoy actual physical contact or are well patterned to cooperate. Other birds also may be interactive but prefer to interact without touching.

✔ Play eye games. Close your eyes, turn away, or otherwise break eye contact until the bird is comfortable looking at you and letting you look back. Look at the bird with only one eye, as another parrot would. Demonstrate that you are not afraid, by blinking while maintaining eye contact. An interested, interactive parrot will close its eyes or blink back.

The Call for Comfort

Candy, a red-lored Amazon, had been through two homes when Karen adopted her. They were devoted to each other, and that's the way things stayed for about 10 years while Karen married and had kids. Then her marriage broke up. It was all she could do to provide for her sons, and Candy was reacting to Karen's stress. The parrot was shredding feathers and calling constantly, a problem that could have cost Karen's family its apartment home.

Karen decided to let Candy stay with a friend who had many birds. Candy grew feathers, called less frequently, and lived happily with "Aunt Vera" until Karen had a house again and could accommodate the bird.

After waiting two years to bring her bird home, Karen was devastated when Candy began chewing feathers and calling incessantly during their first week together. Karen didn't know what to do. The loud calls were making her headachy and irritable. The feather chewing reduced her to tears.

Karen consulted a parrot behavior consultant, who, noting the history of the case, advised her to give Candy lots of interesting toys, warm food, chewable perches, and frequent showers. Karen learned to respond to Candy with quiet words and peekaboos intended to replace her loud calls. These were not established behaviors that had to be ignored, but new/old behaviors that were surfacing because of the stress of moving. They were calls for help or comfort that had to be answered.

Karen played music, sang, and danced with the bird, and within a few days, Candy had abandoned most of those loud calls and discontinued chewing feathers. Within a few weeks, there were lots of other fun new behaviors for Karen to reinforce. By that time, she could merely respond softly to loud calls, and Candy's volume would immediately lower.

✔ Play posture games. Hold still for a long time or crouch over so that you are lower than the bird. Mimic the bird's relaxed or friendly body language. When you see the bird bob or stretch, show it that you feel the same way by exhibiting the same body language. Be careful not to mirror stressed body language.

✔ Play peekaboo around any corner, reading materials, towels, or clothing. Try combining this with the blinking game and the I-can-be-shorter-than-you game.

✔ Play drop-the-toy-and-pick-it-up. This interactive game is frequently initiated by parrots with humans. It's the bird equivalent of "fetch," only the human does the fetching.

✔ Play sound games. Try ringing a bell or tapping from across the room or around a corner when you hear the bird tap or ring a bell. Try to entice the bird to respond to your response.

✔ Wear toys. Arrange to have large buttons, small wooden or plastic toys, bells, or other bird-safe items attached to you or to your clothing. Play with your toys, or have a friend play with your toys, and allow the bird to steal the toys away.

✔ Demonstrate the joys of touching with other humans, pets, or birds. Find a cooperative friend and demonstrate the joys of hugging, cuddling, and petting for the bird. This stimulates cooperation through the use of competition.

✔ Go slowly, and provide lots of delicious foods from the hand.

Step-ups

Look for clues that the bird wants to be touched. Talking, whistling, and other interactive sounds or postures such as lowering the head and ruffling neck feathers or turning the head upside down (exposing the chin) usually indicate a desire to be petted. Try a few head or neck scratches between the cage bars. A bird that is shifting its weight back and forth from one foot to the other and lifting one foot may be asking to be picked up.

If the bird won't step up easily from inside the cage, let it come out on its own. It may step up from the top of the cage or from the cage door. Some birds that stab at or nip a hand that is presented to the front of the foot will cooperate if the hand is presented to the back of the foot.

If the bird won't step up to the hand, try using a hand-held perch or ladder. Take the bird to a small, contained area such as a hallway, laundry room, or closet and try a few slow step-ups to the hand from a chair back or other unfamiliar perch. With the bird sitting on the unfamiliar perch, maintain eye contact and offer a hand to be stepped on, approaching from below to just above the feet. When the bird puts one foot on the hand, continue moving the hand up and toward the bird so that the bird is lifted and the other foot moves also to the hand.

Eye contact is important here. Be sure not to watch your hand as it approaches. If the bird is not watching the approaching hand and is maintaining eye contact, it won't bite. If the bird is watching the approaching hand, distract it by holding an unfamiliar object (anything that the bird isn't terrified of, a spoon or a piece of junk mail) in front of its face. Say *"Step up,"* and move the hand continuously toward the bird's body.

If the bird still won't step up, offer both hands, approaching the feet, from the sides. As the hands come closer together, the bird can choose either one to step on. Some second-hand

When the Bird Is Afraid of a Hand-held Perch

Fear of a stick does not indicate that the bird was hit with a stick. Many parrots, especially older ones, are afraid of sticks, and hand-held perches are sticks. When helping a bird to overcome this fear, put a very short hand-held perch in your pocket, then do a few step-ups from hand to hand in low light and in neutral territory.

Establish a rhythm, and then, maintaining that rhythm, substitute the short perch for one hand. Hold the perch parallel to your index finger and exactly beside the finger, with little or no perch sticking out beyond the finger. As the bird overcomes its fear of the perch, you can use it in many other ways, such as picking the bird up from the cage or a high place you can't reach.

Sometimes a bird that won't step up on a hand or a stick will step up on a dowel ladder. Then the ladder can be used to transition the bird to stepping on hands and hand-held perches.

Eclectus are not generally considered noisy birds. However, they can render an ear shattering scream repeatedly if they think it is the only way they can get their needs met.

hate to be wet, or hate to be handled when wet. If the bird was punished with squirts from a spray bottle, it may be terrified and may require careful strategy to overcome this fear (see page 77).

Patterning

Repeatedly doing enjoyable things with humans establishes a pattern of cooperation in the bird's personality. Any pleasant interaction that can be practiced can be used as patterning. The most common is picking the bird up and putting it down or stepping it from hand to hand in a procedure commonly called a "step-up."

The potentially most difficult step-up is from the cage or home territory. Begin step-up patterning on an unfamiliar perch such as a chair back or sofa. Once the bird is comfortable stepping onto and off an unfamiliar perch, practice stepping it on and off a familiar perch such as the cage.

Be careful not to reinforce unsuccessful interactions. If the bird is not responding, change technique until the bird responds well, or wait until it trusts you more. Some birds that have never successfully learned step-ups or are terrified of human contact may take weeks, months, or even years to step up. Most experienced companion parrots probably will be seeking this type of interaction within a week or two.

Be patient. Cathy Isbel of the Parrot Protection Agency observes that some birds form almost spontaneous bonds in a more suitable new territory, while others take a year or more to really blossom. Even well-adjusted birds improve after being in a new home for a full

birds will step up only on a left hand, others only on a right hand. Reward step-ups or any other behaviors you want to see again with praise such as *"Good bird"* or *"Pretty bird"* or whatever other words the bird responds to favorably.

If the bird likes being misted, it may cooperate with step-ups the first time if it is still wet from a shower. Some birds hate spray baths,

When Loco Met Justus

The yellow-naped Amazon was 15 years old and had a reputation for being mean. People said he could "bite so hard you felt like you had nerve damage." Loco was confined to a small cage, fed an inadequate diet, and had no time out of the cage, and he hadn't had a shower in months. He had chewed his feathers to the down.

Loco had been passed around from one relative to another, and the last one who would have him decided it would be best to have him put to sleep. About that time, Loco met Justus, a young man only a few years older than he. The unwilling caretaker was glad to give Loco to Justus so that she wouldn't have to have the bird euthanized.

Justus put Loco's cage beside his bed, then stayed up and talked to him all night long. Early the next day, Justus opened the cage door, talked a little more, and then put his finger out to see whether Loco would step up. Loco just tucked his head under that finger and ruffled his neck feathers, obviously

Justus and Loco. A second-home bird story with a happy ending!

requesting petting. Justus petted him for a while, then Loco climbed out and got on top of the cage. Justus offered his hand, and Loco stepped up.

They've been buddies ever since. They go on frequent outings, including attending a bird club almost every month.

Unfortunately, Loco doesn't like anyone except Justus. Loco loves to bite Justus's mom, who has to handle him with perches, if at all. Loco has a full set of feathers and a normal range of happiness behaviors, and Mom has adopted a new Quaker named Tequila.

range of seasons. The return of breeding season every year could stimulate bonding with territory, because a wild parrot bonds to the territory it returns to for breeding each year.

Isbel also reports that birds that have been through many homes in a short time take longer to realize that they have finally found a permanent home. New parrot guardians have a better chance of success if they understand that the parrot will eventually accept the new flock and surroundings when it realizes that it has a permanent flock and "territory."

The Towel Game

As quickly as possible, the bird should be socialized to enjoy snuggling and playing in a towel. Because most parrots were hatched and reared in small, dark cavities, they feel safe in small, dark enclosures. Very young parrots often can be carried around nestled in the loose folds of a towel, as one might carry a kitten or a doll.

Because they have been restrained for veterinary examination or grooming, older parrots may actively fear towels or towel restraint. This

How Long Does It Take to Befriend a Parrot?

After living six months in and on a cage in bustling kitchen traffic, Coco, a cherry-headed conure, was biting any hand that reached for her cage. She also frequently climbed to the floor and attacked any toes, human or canine, that she could reach. She was fast. Many toes were nipped, though no blood was ever drawn from a toe. There were dogs and children in the home, and there was concern that an angry shepherd dog might kill the bird.

Dan, a family friend with no other pets, decided to adopt Coco. Although she bit Dan, drawing blood, the first time they met, Dan decided to take Coco as a taming project because she was young and had received excellent care.

A year later, Coco stalked Dan on a regular basis. She obviously hated him. She drew blood at any opportunity, including lunging for his lip twice, resulting in stitches.

Dan, a very organized, goal-oriented person, is known for completing projects on time. He housed the bird low and admitted that he was fixated, perhaps militaristic, in his approach to socializing the little bird. He required Coco to do step-ups, allowing her to bite him repeatedly. Coco would do the step-ups, but she hated interacting with him. He wanted to interact with Coco and did so even when she was biting him.

That approach was too goal-focused for the bird. The patterning process was reinforcing biting, not cooperation.

Luckily, Dan found a parrot behavior consultant who advised shifting gears. Dan had not noticed that Coco loved interacting with him in less confrontational ways. He started playing with the bird more passively. He moved Coco's cage and raised it, and he took the bird on lots of outings in a carrier—all without being bitten once. He looked for opportunities to do things Coco liked. He saw positive changes immediately.

Six months later, Coco likes Dan to scratch her neck through bars. She preens his beard and jumps readily into a towel, then into her carrier, for outings. She loves playing peeka-boo, but she will not allow him to touch her unless there are bars between them. Dan has adjusted to letting Coco guide their interactions. He is gradually convincing her to let him take the lead.

If Dan had been unable to adjust his expectations and behavior, this case might have turned into a matter of incompatibility, and Coco might have lost another home. Companion parrot behavior can't be changed if the humans who care for the birds can't change. Some humans can easily adjust their own behavior, but others cannot.

fear is unnatural, and it can be life-threatening: If towel restraint is highly stressful during medical emergencies, the stress can kill the bird. The towel should be the bird's friend. When the towel is fun, it becomes a versatile tool.

The most dependable early results will probably come from a large towel exactly the color of the bird. A too-small towel or brightly colored or striped fabric frightens some birds. If the bird is terrified of an actual towel, consider using a quilt or down comforter. Don't use knitted or crocheted afghans, because their loose threads can easily snag little toes and cause panic.

Begin by hiding behind the towel and peeking around, over, or under it at the bird. Drape it over your head with the long ends hanging down in front of your shoulders on each side of your face. With the bird perched on a low, free-standing perch or chair back, approach, and lean over the bird. The loose ends of the towel hanging down by the sides of your face will fall forward, forming a cavern containing your head, hands, arms, and shoulders, and, if you are lucky, the bird. You may have to demonstrate this with another pet or a human. The parrot should be curious. Get as close as possible, talking softly to help the bird feel comfortable. Some birds will allow you to get very close, completely enclosing their bodies in the towel. Others may back away until they are more familiar with what is going on.

Eventually, you'll be able to drape the towel completely around the bird, hiding the bird within its folds, and scoop it up. Start "looking" for the bird and playing peekaboo and petting the bird while it is confined within the towel. The bird will become calmer and more receptive during these interactions. This is a great time to practice gently touching the bird. Within a short time, many, but not all, parrots will allow petting of any known-to-be-enjoyable place if only the head or eyes are covered. (Favorite places often include the neck, nostrils, top of the head, area around the eyes, oil gland, wing pit, and hollow under the mandible.)

There is no wrong way to play the towel game if the bird is enjoying it! The goal here is to replicate the feeling of security of being under mommy's wings. If the bird is initially afraid of the towel, try playing with the bird in the covers of your bed. Be sure not to fall asleep when playing snuggle games with the bird in your bed, because the bird could easily suffocate if it crawls into the wrong position.

The Bird with No Name

He'd already killed one mate and injured a second when the breeder phoned to ask if I knew anyone who would like to keep a large male Umbrella cockatoo as a companion. The bird had been caged with PVC perches, no toys, and no access to anything chewable, except, of course, himself and his mate. Thought to be a teenager, he would bite any human whenever possible, and with a developing reputation as a mate murderer, his future probably depended upon his ability to adjust as a companion.

The bird that is now called Joey was adopted by Sharona, a spiritual older woman, a minister and a psychic, who now handles him like a teddy bear. He still attacks other people (except his behaviorist) and any shoes or feet he can reach.

It took Sharona a few weeks to learn to handle the large bird in a towel and to play towel games. Once the human got the hang of the towel game, the bird was as good as tame. Joey loves to be petted, but likes to solicit intimate pats under the wing. Sharona, his loving guardian of eight years, knows to pet him on the head, jaw, neck, beak, nostrils, skin around the beak, tongue, and eye rings rather than on the back under the wings, which obviously stimulates him sexually. He and Sharona even survived a fire, fleeing in the night with a cat in another carrier.

Bringing a second-hand parrot into your home can be extremely rewarding, but it's not always easy. This chapter explores ways to deal with difficult behaviors so the transition will be as smooth as possible.

Talking

Many parrots find their way into human hearts because they vocalize, but there are two sides to that coin. More second-hand parrots lose their homes for excessive vocalization than for any other reason. Only a small part of parrot talk is low-volume vocalization. A parrot's wild language is intended to share information. Wake-up calls, come-to-dinner calls, alarm calls, and everybody-come-to-roost calls must be loud enough for all to hear.

Long, loud calls are intended to get a response, any response. As a result, these calls are often accidentally reinforced. Humans must learn to divert the birds to different behaviors.

Volume might not be the only problem. Second-hand parrots come into a new home saying what they heard in earlier homes. Neither foul language nor foul sounds are unusual.

It might take a while to start understanding what the bird is saying. Some of the fun of

Second-home birds often surprise their owners with their repertoire of words and tricks. (Scarlet macaw)

living with a second-hand parrot is discovering in the bird's vocabulary words and phrases that you don't use. A bird that says only a dozen or so words on a regular basis may suddenly come out with an entire sentence or phrase.

Many parrots can associate the words they use with their meanings, and they often improvise their own meanings for words. Sometimes they improvise a word for a meaning.

Learning New Words

Many people think that older birds don't learn new words readily. It's a matter of motivation, however. A young bird has fun talking, whether it gets a response or not. As the bird gets older, it's the response that counts. When the guardian stops responding, the bird stops talking. An older bird will be less likely to look for things that get a response.

When a talking parrot moves to a happier home, it is motivated to acquire the language of the new flock. Once the bird realizes that talking is rewarded with food and fun interactions, the vocabulary begins to grow, with new words appearing often.

Scarlet Improvises

Scarlet, a found macaw, loved to reach down with her giant beak, pinch a forearm (hard!), scream "Ouch!" and laugh maniacally. She would stab any living creature just to see if it would jump. It was easy to take advantage of this love of drama.

Early on, I started screaming "Ouch" and jumping at times when she was not nipping or stabbing. I would touch her tail or body and scream "Ouch" dramatically.

Within weeks, Scarlet learned that she could get "Ouch" from me anytime she wanted, just by touching me. Within a month, I could offer her a finger, and she would hold it gently in her beak, and we would scream "Ouch" together, then laugh. She replaced her biting for drama with acted-out drama. She also discovered many associated ways to use that word she likes so much.

One day, I watched Scarlet playing the ouch game with her perch. She would touch it with her beak and then scream "Ouch!" and laugh an almost human laugh. Later, she learned to use that same word when she experienced pain. I first heard this when she flew against a wall.

Another day (after she'd had to give a blood sample), she stayed in her cage and slept, saying "Scarlet, ouch" quietly when invited out. She seemed to be using "Ouch" to say "I don't feel good."

Still later, Scarlet learned to use the word when she was afraid of something. Lately, she's begun saying "Ouch" if I try to make her step up onto an unfamiliar perch, as if using that same word to mean, "I don't want to!"

Vocalizations Aren't Always Sweet and Low

Most parrots, like most humans, have the ability to be at least occasionally loud, but the redundant use of excessively loud calls can be habitual. A parrot's experiences influence its vocal behaviors. From the moment a parrot is aware of its surroundings, interesting tools (toys) must be provided to stimulate self-rewarding (play) behaviors. If a parrot does not learn to amuse itself, no amount of ignoring attention-demanding calls will silence it.

A bird must have a workable way to call the flock. Screaming is the natural thing to try first. In most homes, screaming gets attention eventually. Often, ignoring the screaming makes the bird more insecure and more frantic to get the flock's attention, so it screams louder. If the flock can choose a call that is more pleasant and answer that call reliably, the bird will use the new call instead of screaming. *Peekaboo's* and elongated *Helloooo's* or *Hola's* are good replacement calls to verify contact. At first the bird may use the new call often. When it is satisfied that the new quiet call works and always gets a response, there will be less need to use it. The bird will become more secure and quieter.

Attention-demanding calls are used more often when the bird's emotional or physical needs are not met. If the bird relies too much on a human for security and entertainment, it will feel abandoned if the person even leaves the room. The bird will do whatever it takes to get the human's attention. A parrot's instinct is to call longer and louder until it is answered.

Replacing unwanted calls entails convincing the bird that some other call is more fun and

A Behavioral Emergency

His neighbor had gone out of town for the weekend, leaving him to baby-sit a hen cockatiel. Within 48 hours, Feather (his only bird, a beautiful red-tailed grey parrot) would utter no sound except the loud alarm signal of the female cockatiel.

Stepping off the elevator, I could hear the shrieking call from outside the closed door at the end of the hallway. It was the most excruciatingly annoying hen-cockatiel "Chirp!" I had ever heard, at about three times normal cockatiel volume.

Remaining out of the bird's sight, I asked, "How long has this been going on?"

"Well, this is Wednesday," Feather's human companion replied in a whisper, obviously terrified that he would be living with this for the rest of his life. "I baby-sat my neighbor's cockatiel over the weekend. It started Monday morning, and I called you before noon that day."

"Ahh, we should be able to fix this pretty easily, then. Please bring me two solid-colored towels, preferably gray."

Entering the room, we were careful not to look at the bird when it chirped for attention. We sat across from each other. Draping large gray terrycloth towels over our heads, we obscured our faces, then spent 30 or 40 minutes playing peekaboo with the towels, around the corners of the room, and from behind plants and the furniture.

Feather was baffled. He immediately discontinued that newly acquired chirp. Within 15 minutes, he was calling out trial words like "Hello" and "What?" in an effort to participate in the game. By the next morning, Feather had figured out how to say "Peekaboo," and for a few days, he replaced all vocalizations with that one very exciting phrase.

Because we worked on the newly acquired behavior immediately and very dramatically, our efforts were completely successful. Feather never again shrieked like a cockatiel, but tried, whenever possible, to engage willing humans in peeking games.

more useful. When replacement behaviors are planned for, stimulated, and reinforced, screaming behaviors quickly subside. Playing peekaboo and calling the bird's name can stimulate rewardable behaviors. When the bird is rewarded for the new behavior quickly and consistently but is never rewarded for screaming, it replaces screaming with the new behavior. As the bird feels increasingly secure, it develops more independent habits.

Many second-hand birds come into new homes after having their most basic needs neglected. If the bird lived in a busy human traffic area, it may not have had sufficient sleep. Often, because the bird has been neither allowed out of the cage for a long time nor bathed frequently, its needs for exercise have also been neglected. A bird that has too much energy from lack of bathing and exercise and is cranky because it hasn't had enough sleep is likely to vocalize loudly. A bird that hasn't had enough sleep might benefit from a roost cage. If a bird starts screaming at midday for no apparent reason, and the screaming goes on

Recognizing an aggressive posture is often the first step in avoiding a bite. This African grey is defending his perch. It might be best to pick him up with a hand-held perch.

Not all loud vocalizations can be eliminated. Many birds feel they must scream when anybody comes home—friend, foe, or stranger. Early morning and evening calls can be important and irreplaceable. You can manipulate early morning screaming by covering the cage or providing a roost cage in a room that can remain dark until humans awake. Some early morning screamers can be pacified by placing yummy food treats in their bowls in the dark during the night so that they can find and enjoy a treat before the cage is uncovered in the morning.

If you can't work things out with help from this text and from *Guide to Companion Parrot Behavior*, it's a good idea to seek immediate professional help. Parrot volume can be turned down most easily if annoying new vocalizations are addressed quickly. Behavioral programs are usually designed to replace unwanted vocalizations with different behaviors. Sometimes those replacement behaviors are other vocalizations, sometimes they are altogether different behaviors, such as chewing, playing, bathing, or napping.

for more than 20 minutes, you might try putting it in the roost cage or covering the day cage and setting a timer for a 20-minute nap. Note the time the screaming incident occurred, and put the bird down for a nap just before that time the next day, so that you will have anticipated and prevented a repetition of the unwanted behavior.

Some birds are jealous of the attention the other flock members give the television or the telephone. They scream loudly to compete. Try giving the bird a special toy or treat before turning on the television or while on the way to answering the phone. A teaspoonful of finch seed can keep a large bird busy for long enough to have a phone conversation. Eventually, the bird will be satisfied with using an established contact call or signal call a few times during a conversation or program. As long as the person talking or watching takes a second to answer, the bird will feel secure and scream less. (Please note that this doesn't mean the bird will not scream at all.)

Nipping and Biting

Many humans are simply not emotionally equipped to cope with having pain inflicted by a companion animal. Biting (a behavior intended to damage) is probably the second most common reason parrots are passed to new homes. Typically, it isn't possible to determine why a parrot was biting in its previous home(s). Further, it doesn't matter why the bird bit in the old home, because the new home brings opportunities for new behaviors.

Parrots interacting with each other will nip (a practice intended to influence behavior, but not to damage) and pull feathers to communicate boundaries that they set with each other. Disapproval is exhibited clearly, often including vocal admonitions. Nips are part of a parrot's natural communication, especially in defining territory. It isn't possible, or even desirable, to eliminate this nipping.

A nip is not a bite. A bite typically breaks the skin or leaves a significant bruise. That goes beyond simple communication and often involves a fear response, a game, or a state of extreme excitement.

Fear, Aggression, or Fun?

Often, a parrot's bite hurts the person's feelings more than it hurts the person's flesh. It's easy to get the notion that the parrot is being "mean." Because parrots are wild animals, with all of their instincts intact, fear and aggression can occur simultaneously. A parrot may bite because it fears it is in danger, or it may be defending a mate, offspring, or territory from a rival. The bird defends those things because it instinctively knows that they are necessary to be successful, that is, to raise offspring. A parrot that seems to hate an individual or an entire gender is acting out a rivalry.

Many birds will defend a high perch. This Double Yellow-headed Amazon's raised head feathers and pinning eyes indicate an excited bird that would probably bite.

Avoiding Being Bitten

✔ Don't stick fingers in a bird's cage.
✔ Don't try to pick a bird up when it's eating or playing actively.
✔ Prompt for the step-up on the lowest part of the belly near the legs.
✔ Avoid holding fingers in the bite zone, the area in front of and near the face.
✔ Don't pick up a bird that is displaying and showing off.
✔ Believe a bird's warning that it will bite. Pick up such a bird with a hand-held perch instead of fingers. If the bird is in a cage, try letting it come out first.
✔ Distract the bird's eyes from the approaching hand.
✔ Offer the whole hand for a bird to step onto instead of one or two fingers.
✔ Don't allow a parrot to establish territory on the floor, lest it learn to stalk toes.

The Con Artist

After two years in his current home, Ernie, a 17-year-old Goffin's cockatoo, and his humans had reached an understanding. They could interact without touching. They could dance and flirt, wink and blink, and many happiness behaviors appeared in both humans and bird.

However, if humans fell for the look of longing in the bird's eyes, ruffled neck feathers, arched neck, and upturned chin, and if they came close enough to touch the bird, he would quickly turn and slash skin with obvious delight. No amount of warning could save headstrong humans who were sure their reflexes were quicker than the bird's. Inevitably, even the most experienced and knowledgeable human would succumb to the feathered con artist.

Ernie's guardian, a veterinarian, wanted to know how to get the bird past this most unlovable habit and knew that Ernie was terrified of towels. Most Goffin's cockatoos can just play the towel game, get petted all over, and learn that being petted is more fun than watching people bleed and jump and scream. Because Ernie was afraid of towels, however, nobody knew what to do next, so a parrot behavior consultant was called.

Mattie Sue arrived looking like a Halloween ghost, completely covered by a quilt. Ernie's family spent five or ten sweltering minutes under the quilt with her until the curious bird climbed down off his cage and walked over to get under the quilt with them. Mattie Sue taught Ernie to snuggle and get petted in the quilt without biting. Ernie's guardian got a quilt and petted him past his biting game.

Six months later, Ernie has feathers on what were bare legs. He goes to bird club and plays with strangers. He spends his days on the counter at the veterinarian's office, throwing pens and papers on the floor for adoring humans to pick up.

A heightened state of excitement will also cause a bird to bite. This wound-up behavior is notorious in Amazons and cockatoos, but it can be seen in other parrots as well. Becoming aggressive with an aggressive bird complicates things. Interact with the bird only in ways that do not stimulate biting. If the bite is avoided, it cannot be reinforced into a pattern.

Parrots, particularly young ones, like to chew on whatever they are standing on. Sometimes there doesn't seem to be anything else to do while sitting on someone's hand. If these nips get a reaction from the person, then the reaction functions as a reward to the bird. Because the bird was looking for fun, a person who is jumping around and squealing often fits the bill. Suddenly the bird is biting because it can create excitement and fun.

Preventing Biting

Keep a bird from biting by avoiding the situations that result in the bird's need to bite. With fearful birds, go slowly enough that the bird doesn't feel threatened. With hormonal birds, keep the bird's attention diverted and put it back in the cage before it gets too excited. Do not pull a finger out of a bird's mouth once it has latched on. (Pulling away in the middle of a bite will result in loss of flesh.)

Forcing a frightened bird out of a cage can result in biting. Try getting the bird out by more passive means, such as putting the cage on the floor with the opening on top. That will sometimes encourage the bird to crawl out. Once the bird is out, offer it both hands to step onto, one on each side. If the bird still isn't ready to stand on a hand, encourage it to step onto a hand-held perch or ladder.

A territorial bird will be most cooperative in neutral territory. A bird may claim a certain person as a mate substitute or territory and bite if a rival approaches. In this case, have a private time with the bird when the rival won't show up unexpectedly.

There may be times when the bird is more easily excited. Watch for such times and be willing to put the bird away before it loses self-control. Keep the bird occupied with hand-held toys. Singing songs and playing talking games may be too stimulating while the bird is on your hand. Calm scratching of the head without touching the sides of the beak or back under the wings may be acceptable interaction.

If the bird is jumping off the play area or the top of the cage to attack a person (rival), restrict access to those areas. Trim the bird's wing feathers so that it can't stalk by flying.

Anticipate, Distract, Reinforce

Anything that the bird has done once can be reinforced. Life is fun, and all creatures prefer to do things they enjoy. Because almost any nonviolent interaction with a human can be interpreted by the bird as reinforcement, take

What Do You Do if the Bird's Beak Is Around Your Flesh, Biting You?

Of course, the best way to deal with biting is to prevent it, but if all efforts have failed and you are looking down at a parrot that is lacerating your flesh and unwilling to quit, what do you do?

If the bird is sitting on your other hand or on a perch, it's fairly easy to get the bird to release by pushing the hand being bitten toward the bird. Of course, anyone who knows how human reflexes work probably knows that most humans experiencing a painful bite want to pull their hand away. A human who pulls away runs the risk of ripping flesh, injuring the bird, or actually teaching the bird to bite by a response that reinforces the behavior.

If the bird is sitting on your hand, distract it with a gentle wobble. If it is not on your hand, distract it by waving a foreign object near its eyes. Put the bird quickly, gently, and unceremoniously on the floor or into the cage. Some birds will release if light-blocking fabric is placed over their heads. If the bird is hanging on and grinding, you might try forcing something else into the beak, letting it bite down on a magazine or a handy pair of glasses instead.

Eye contact is really important here, for if you can catch the bird's eye, it will usually release your hand. An improvised distraction may be necessary to change a determined bird's focus on the bite. That could mean clapping the other hand against your thigh or suddenly turning the television volume up with the remote.

When the bird is biting a finger, it is best to push the finger back toward the bird rather than pulling it away.

care not to allow unwanted behaviors to occur. For example, if the bird is nipping in response to a particular set of interactions, redesign the way those interactions are performed. If the bird is nipping hands as it comes off the cage, you might temporarily step-up the bird off the cage onto hand-held perches. If you have properly patterned cooperation into your birds, you might use good hand/bad hand (distract the bird's eyes just before giving the step-up command), or you might have the bird step up onto towel-covered hands.

It's quite common to reinforce behavior accidentally, especially in a creature that is looking for any kind of attention (reward). Even saying "No" can provide drama for an excitement-starved little parrot. A normal, creative parrot that has learned to anticipate praise (reward) for good behavior usually becomes more willing to seek new ways to generate rewards. The bird will also gradually abandon behaviors that fail to bring at least occasional reinforcement.

Punishments and Quick Fixes

Because of its sensitive nature and well-developed fear response, there is no effective punishment for a parrot. The bird's natural instinct to avoid danger must be respected. Both punishments and reprimands are so counterproductive that even the mildest ones are to be avoided. A nipping parrot is not to be dropped, forcefully squirted, thumped on the beak, isolated in a scary place, or hit in any way. Even if a reprimand temporarily or permanently causes the bird to discontinue biting, the potential for harming the bird or the human/bird bond is real. A bird that is punished might never again trust humans.

In the long run, reprimands don't work. Distracting to appropriate behavior and positive reinforcement are the best means of modifying unwanted parrot behavior and the easiest way to train a parrot. Such techniques are often used successfully though humans may be unaware of what they are doing. It's just as common for someone to be accidentally reinforcing good behaviors as to be accidentally reinforcing unwanted ones.

Even step-ups can be a quick fix if they are done only occasionally. Although parrot behavior usually isn't permanently changed by stimulating a one-time behavioral change, the benefit of an immediate change can be the turning point for the humans who create the bird's environment. Because it's difficult to change human behavior, anything that safely generates a one-time change in the bird can demonstrate what it is capable of, and that may be the best way to convince humans that if they change, the bird will also change.

The Fearful Parrot

When confronted with an unfamiliar and therefore potentially dangerous situation, a bird's first response is to fight or flee. This is called the fight-or-flight response. This fear response, as we might put it, can contribute to behavioral reactions such as biting (the "fight" part of the fight-or-flight response), alarm calls, thrashing, falling, inability to regrow repeatedly knocked-out wing or tail feathers, and even self-inflicted feather damage.

Repeated fear responses place stress on both the bird and the people who live with it. A fearful parrot is at risk of being isolated and neglected by humans for any of the unwanted behaviors associated with fearfulness. Isolated, neglected parrots are prime candidates for new homes; indeed, a new home is a thoughtful, compassionate solution if isolation and neglect are the only alternatives. But a fearful bird can be bounced from home to home year after year just as surely as a screaming one.

Whether the response to a fearful situation is to bite (fight) or escape (flee), once a behavior has been repeatedly enacted and reinforced, it stands a chance of becoming habitual and a permanent feature of the bird's behavior. The fight-or-flight response is designed to remove the bird from danger. In captivity, the bird often cannot escape the perceived danger, which frightens it even more. That cycle can result in a bird that is afraid of being afraid, and so is prone to frequent panic attacks.

A fearful bird may benefit from having a small cage, possibly protected on the sides with a cage cover.

A sensitive bird can easily develop fearful responses to severe grooming, inappropriate housing, large, slick perches, unsteady perches, exposed cages, too-small cages, too-large cages, or almost anything else in the environment that stimulates stress. Even boredom, encountered at just the wrong time, can induce or heighten fear reactions in a companion parrot. A new, enhanced environment creates opportunities for new, confident behaviors to develop.

Some birds benefit from having a plant or other low barrier between the cage and the activity beyond the cage. Others enjoy having a box to hide in or having a towel obscuring part of the cage for a few days, sometimes longer.

Trying to remove a shy or fearful bird from the cage by force can stimulate and reinforce panic and harm the human/bird relationship. A bird with sensitive new wing feathers growing in may react adversely. The frightened bird may bite or fall, breaking the feather it was protecting. Then the bird becomes so evasive and protective of wings that it may panic and automatically jump or thrash the next time it sees the human involved, or any other human. That sets the bird up for fear of falling and fear of humans.

Let a new second-hand parrot that is known to bite or thrash come out of the cage on its own. Then the bird can learn to step up in neutral territory before learning to step up from the cage door or cage top. A fearful bird needs to know that the inside of the cage is sacred, that nobody will intrude into bird space. Never require such a bird to be handled, though you might sometimes trick a shy bird into coming out of the cage by removing the bottom tray and grate and gently turning the cage upside down.

Fear and the Environment

A bird that is not stimulated to play is not curious, and a bird that is not curious is more likely to exhibit increasingly self-centered behaviors, including skittishness or fearfulness. Additionally, a parrot kept in a poorly designed or badly located cage with insufficient light, inadequate diet, or insufficient sleep will be more inclined to resort to fear responses.

Make sure that most of the bird's perches, including the main perch where it spends most of its time, are small enough to be gripped securely. If the bird is startled and flaps, but cannot grip the perch it is sitting on, it can easily fall. Failure of confidence can develop in a bird that falls often. An overly cautious parrot can sit around and gradually become less and less interested in diverse activities and more and more easily frightened by almost anything.

The more the bird is exposed to sensitive handling and an interesting, diverse environment, the more likely it is that curiosity and exploration will dominate the bird's behaviors, rather than caution or fearfulness. If a newly relocated parrot is going through a clumsy or shy phase, or if the bird is growing a set of (uncomfortable) new wing feathers, it should not be handled by inexperienced or unfamiliar humans.

Building Trust

A program to modify established fearfulness will require gradual reinforcement of small changes in order to achieve long-range goals. Fearful behaviors can be successfully replaced with other behaviors in many cases, however. If the bird was in a scary place with people who didn't understand how to make it feel more comfortable, then the perceived paradise of the new environment can easily stimulate new, less-fearful behaviors. As we replace fearful behaviors with others that are more useful in companion settings, the old behaviors will occur less and less frequently. If we replace enough of the fear responses with more useful responses, then gradually the fear responses will become obsolete.

Established fearfulness in a mature parrot can be extremely difficult to change. First, win the bird's trust with good food, good perches, baths, routine, and a sense of safety fostered by consistently unintrusive human behavior. Let the bird watch you put yummy treats into the bowl with your hand. If it will take food from you, share as much warm food—a parrot's equivalent of loving comfort—as possible.

Some parrots that do not tolerate physical contact prefer to interact with humans in other ways. It's a real advantage to know how to connect emotionally without actually touching the bird. Look for ways in which the bird wants to interact with you. These various interactions might include eye games, body language games, and other types of play that involve no physical contact (see Interacting Without Touching, page 61).

Demonstrate affectionate behavior with other humans, pets, or birds. Find a cooperative friend or loved one who likes to be hugged and touched and petted, and demonstrate the joys of hugging, touching, and petting for the bird. If the bird can be easily moved to a carrier, new bonds can be forged with familiar humans in unfamiliar locations. Sometimes just taking the bird for a ride in the car will generate noticeable improvements, even if the bird is never removed from the carrier. The bird enjoys a new, enhanced experience and comes home safely, with an improved sense of security.

Establish routine where possible. Any time the bird can anticipate pleasant events, fear will be reduced. Try starting the day with a simple routine. (Complex routines are difficult to maintain.) Announce intentions in advance: "I'm going to turn the music on now."

Say *"Step-up"* before picking the bird up, even if it cooperates without the verbal prompt. Say *"Scratch"* or *"Tickle"* before petting the bird. Knowing what will happen next prevents fear responses. Tell the bird what's going to happen *before* a hand (or spray bottle, or food dish) approaches. The more predictable the human is, the more the bird will trust that person, and the less fear the bird will experience around that person.

The development of a confident relationship with a human can be a major breakthrough, because a bird may then develop more confidence in all areas of behavior, including new, more-trusting relationships with other humans.

Growing Feathers

Just as feather-damaging behaviors may appear with the stress of changing homes, feather-damaging behaviors may disappear as the bird realizes the benefits of its new home. A feather that was pulled out can regrow in four to six weeks. A feather that has been damaged cannot grow in until what remains of it falls out, a process called molting. New blood feathers come in encased in sheaths of protein similar to fingernail cuticle. The bird removes this cuticle during preening. The sheath gradually dries out and flakes off as the feather opens up from the tip.

Parrots molt at different times of the year, depending upon their natural breeding cycles and other environmental factors. Some parrots molt quickly, some more slowly, some molt almost continuously. The molt begins at the head, which may appear to be covered in spikes. These are new feathers with the sheaths still intact. A human or bird companion might help the bird to get those feather sheaths off, but many high-strung parrots won't allow it. Increasing showers from twice weekly to every day will help the bird to complete the molting process.

As the molt progresses, there will be obvious accumulations of feathers to be regularly vacuumed. Young, active birds may replace every feather every year. Mature birds may take two or three molts before all of the feathers are

replaced. In this time, the old feathers can become visibly worn. A bird that has suffered ongoing stress, especially ongoing nutritional stress, may begin worrying, overpreening, or overtly damaging feathers. Old, worn-out, unmolted, or damaged feathers can therefore induce self-inflicted damage to the feathers. All efforts should be made to replace the old feather-damaging behaviors before the new feathers grow in. Progress will be visible as the molt progresses.

Feather-Growing Checklist

1. Allow the bird to experience natural day length, putting it to bed at sundown rather than artificially limiting the experience of daylight hours to the time when humans have the lights on. Use common sense, be moderate. Try to approximate the daylight cycles that the bird's wild ancestors might have experienced.

Provide bright natural, bright fluorescent, or full-spectrum lighting.

2. Allow the bird to experience natural fluctuations in temperature. A cage in an unair-conditioned or unheated part of the home or a room where central air and heat are closed off can allow a healthy bird to safely experience seasonal temperatures between 50 and 90°F (10–32°C).

3. Be sure that the bird has adequate opportunities for stimulating its metabolism with exercise. Give it adequate access to moisture in the form of baths and showers, because recovering from being wet is a form of exercise for a companion parrot. Encourage exercise beyond what the bird chooses to do on its own.

4. Be sure that the bird learns both independent and cooperative behaviors. A stimulating environment can help to ensure that a particular bird needs less, rather than more, human attention.

5. Especially if there are feather problems, this is a good time for that veterinary checkup. If there are minor physical problems, clearing them up at this time can contribute to healthy preening behaviors rather than feather-damaging behaviors.

6. Improve nutrition. Provide lots of stimulating, healthful, fresh foods to supplement a balanced, nutritionally complete pelleted diet. Some birds, especially older birds with slow molt, benefit from the addition of iodine-rich foods to the diet. Try adding a little kelp or fish

A collar may help a bird start growing its feathers back while problems in the environment are corrected. It may also help break the cycle if the picking has become habitual.

oil. Don't supplement vitamins without veterinary supervision; that could kill the bird.

7. Use filtered or bottled water for the bird's bath and drinking water. Some public water supplies are overtreated or may have unsafe organisms during times of runoff.

8. Customize grooming. Be sure nails are sharp enough to enable secure gripping and short enough to keep from getting caught on elements of the environment. Especially long, curved nails can cause stress by interfering with climbing. Allow wing feathers to grow out completely if the home can be made safe for a flying bird.

9. Provide diverse perches set at angles. Small perches provide gripping opportunities, adding confidence by preventing falls and the stress that accompanies falling.

10. Provide many destructible items, such as paper, cardboard, and fabric, which the bird can readily destroy.

11. If the bird has been wearing a device to prevent feather damage, ask the veterinarian or behaviorist monitoring progress when to remove the device. Depending upon the bird, the best time is probably when there are many nearly mature new feathers that need to be cleaned and preened. If the bird is putting in new feathers quickly enough, appropriate

All parrots (like this Hyacinth macaw) need human stimulation and training.

Chewed or Snapped Feather has no base

Molted Feather has a base, even if it is very small (down)

preening behaviors can replace feather-damaging behaviors. The bird may have to be misted several times daily if feather damage is being perpetrated on dry feathers. Usually, if the damaging behaviors can be stopped for 28 days without a device, the bird doesn't have to be misted as much after that. If damaging behaviors come in a predictable cycle, then the device might be replaced during times when the bird is likely to damage feathers.

12. Many new behaviors must be provided to replace the old behaviors. This might mean more human attention or a more stimulating environment. Sometimes a TV does wonders here, but don't forget simple things like fresh twigs or branches (or pieces of wadded-up paper) stuck through the bars of the cage or laid on top of the cage. A curious bird will try to pull them into the cage or knock them off the cage.

Evaluating Progress

Human memory sometimes plays tricks. Progress can be seen most easily by taking photos about once weekly. If you are still finding feathers on the bottom of the cage, put them into an envelope, date it, and chart the number of feathers damaged each day to observe a trend.

The cycle of feather damage can begin again when the molt is ended. If the bird can grow feathers during one molting season and retain them until the next, then the feather-damaging behaviors can be considered cured. Damaging behaviors may reappear in times of stress or illness.

For more specific or detailed instructions on the treatment of this and other established behavior problems, see *Guide to a Well-Behaved Parrot, Guide to Companion Parrot Behavior, Guide to the Quaker Parrot, Guide to the Senegal Parrot and Its Family,* and *The African Grey Parrot Handbook.*

The Tattooed Parrot

A sensitive parrot may respond to almost anything by damaging its feathers. Whether this behavior relates to illness, diet, aggressive handling, perceived threat, perceived abandonment, wing trim, dietary reactions, or any of a multitude of other contributing factors, it can destroy the beauty of the bird's feathers. Beauty is only skin deep, however, and some of the best-loved, most famous parrots in the world damage their own feathers.

That may not mean that the bird is neurotic. Like the Doctor's naked parrot in Gabriel García Márquez' *Love in the Time of Cholera,* not every human who chews his or her fingernails is neurotic. That bird was certainly not neurotic, and it was said that the Doctor loved the bird more than his own children.

Not every bird that chews its feathers is unhappy. Feather-damaging behaviors may be habitual or related to the bird's physiology. Sometimes they can be changed, sometimes they can't.

Some birds chew feathers once, recover, then never chew them again. Others, like Alex, the famous African grey, and Mattie Sue's own Portia, chew and then recover in a physical or circumstantial cycle. Those birds' guardians love them unequivocally, for what they are, for who they are, and not for what they look like.

Loving humans often react emotionally when they perceive that their birds are chewing, snapping, or plucking out their own feathers. At first, it's easy to feel overwhelmed by guilt whenever you look at the bird. Many people cry and decide that they are not good for the bird. Some heartbroken guardians of feather-damaging birds, for better or worse, give them away.

But is that really a mature reaction? Most loving humans go the extra mile to find out what's going on, so that the behavior can be remedied. Do everything possible to ensure that the bird isn't ill or physically uncomfortable.

Once the behaviors have been present for a while, we realize that the bird is still the same bird. It still walks and talks and plays and loves us and depends on us for everything necessary to survive, every drop of water, every morsel of food. If the bird is loved less for its appearance, then we have let it down. Accepting a feather-chewing bird and loving it unequivocally, in the home in which the feather chewing developed, can be a profound and sometimes spiritual process. At what point did the wives, mothers, and lovers of Michael Jordan, Yul Brynner, and Telly Savalas realize that handsome, for their men, meant bald?

Some people respond to the first sight of a beloved feather-chewing parrot with shock. That reaction can't be helped, but criticism is inappropriate. It's no more appropriate to criticize a hard-working, compassionate parrot guardian who is unable to stop his or her bird from damaging feathers than it is to criticize the parent of a young adult with tattoos or piercings.

A feather-chewing bird is demonstrating the control it has over its own body, an urge that cannot be denied. Many guardians have gone the extra mile to help their birds overcome this ugly habit. More than that, however, they have stayed with the bird, loved and nurtured it, kept it in spite of ridicule and guilt. They deserve commendation, not judgment.

Caring humans who are well bonded to their birds don't casually give up a companion parrot because of perceived behavior problems. Nobody's perfect, however, and nothing stays the same.

In most lives, there will come a time when caring for birds is no longer an option. The bird's best interests must be protected. If the bird is no longer receiving good care, and if care cannot be improved in its current home, then it's time to look for a new home.

Advancing age: Although many assisted-living facilities and nursing homes now allow a new resident to bring one small bird, it may not be feasible to continue caring for a bird when one can no longer care for oneself.

It takes only a short time for a bird to die of thirst. If a parrot's guardian is physically challenged and lives alone, try to establish a daily checkup system so that someone knows that all is well until a suitable home can be found for the bird. This procedure, necessary for anyone who lives alone, can ensure that the bird will be found if the guardian falls ill or dies. A checkup service might be provided through a bird club or a church support group. It is a noble and worthy project that may involve no more than

Unlike young cockatoos, juvenile Timneh greys are rarely available second-hand.

a daily telephone call to ensure that the care-giver is still able to provide for the bird.

Illness, including drug or alcohol addiction. Some illnesses, even severe ones, are transitory; others are not. If there is reason to believe that a caring guardian will recover, then temporary placement might be considered.

Anger-management issues: If violence in the home has been directed to clothing or other nonliving objects, then a small companion animal may be the next target in this often escalating and progressive disorder. Birds are common victims of domestic violence. Get the bird out quickly, even if you have to take it to a foster home or a shelter. Alternatively, ask a neighbor to keep it for a few days. Seek professional help immediately. Temporary placement might be an option, because humans may also be in danger and unable to stay in an angry home.

When the lives or relationships of established flock mates are compromised by the new bird: Not every adoption placement can be successful. Every effort should be made to anticipate foreseeable complications, but if the lives of established birds, pets, or people in the home are challenged, then the bird must be returned or placed in another home.

If the bird is absolutely incompatible with a vulnerable family member such as a child: This behavior can be a natural part of a bird's instinctual behaviors that tell it to challenge flock members that seem weak or unfamiliar and to drive them away from the flock. A fully functioning, emotionally balanced adult can easily cope with something resembling hatred from a bird, but a young, very elderly, handicapped, or otherwise challenged human may not be able to easily cope with the bird's behavior. The time to find a new home for the bird has come.

Direct Placement

Most caring bird guardians probably feel most confident about a beloved companion parrot's new home when they are able to select it themselves. Of course, it's easier to stay in touch if a new home can be found in one's regular circle of friends, family, or coworkers. Bird clubs and their events can also provide opportunities to find compatible situations for companion parrots.

Most second-hand bird placements probably are made through newspaper classified sections. Whether it's a large-city daily or a classified weekly, there will be many ads. An accurate description of the bird and its species can prevent calls from unsuitable situations.

Evaluating the New Home

The needs and characteristics of the bird will determine the home into which the bird should go. The new guardian should be equipped to

deal with existing behavior problems. Birds that seem unable to make the adjustment to life as a companion parrot should not be placed in breeder programs. This disposition could be

Survival Story

Ann Hartmann seemed young for 70. She did a great job caring for her flock of five lories, a canary-winged bee bee, and Molly, a Moluccan cockatoo. Because Ann had belonged to an active bird club for many years and was well aware that her parrots could outlive her, she had done a good job of estate planning. She'd made provisions to leave a home unencumbered by mortgage, and an insurance trust sufficient to pay taxes and insurance and maintain her collection of birds. And she'd found a niece willing to take on those responsibilities.

Because she seemed so young and active, Mrs. Hartmann didn't expect to go suddenly. One month, she didn't show up for bird club, and one of the other members decided to stop by her home to deliver some toys ordered through the club co-op. Ann Hartmann had been dead for more than a week. The small birds were lost, but the Moluccan cockatoo had survived by cannibalizing her own breast.

Ten years later, Molly lives happily in a new home, but still occasionally chews her breast and breast feathers. She has learned to wear a bandanna in public to distract her from self-damaging behavior. She's sweet to everyone, not excessively noisy, and practically worshipped by the family she lives with now. Although they've done everything they could to remedy her behavioral maladjustments, they don't mind that her appearance isn't perfect.

passed on to future generations. There are sanctuaries where such birds can live out their lives. There are also some individuals who will take good care of a bird in spite of its poor pet quality.

Ideally, the guardian giving up the bird should know as much as possible about its new home, and the new guardian should know as much as possible about the bird's history. There should be a written record of the bird's habits, likes, and dislikes, in addition to a health and medical history.

Consignment

Occasionally, a retail birdseller will have developed a market for second-hand birds. It's unusual, and it's a little tricky, because baby birds should be kept separate from second-hand birds, which may expose them to physical and behavioral complications.

A consignment store might have a well-prepared pool of potential guardians who appreciate a larger selection from which to choose a good match. It can have a downside, for example, when a bird that learned to cuss in its previous home teaches profane words to other birds.

Consignment organizations are best screened as carefully as new guardians, but additional information is needed to decide whether to leave the bird for sale in a retail setting. Documentation is especially important here. Be sure that the organization has a written agreement designating the responsibilities of the temporary care provider. Be sure that an agreement covers quarantine and specifies who is responsible for medical care if the bird falls ill. It should also state who is responsible if the bird

Questions to Ask Potential New Guardians
- ✔ Have you lived with a bird before?
- ✔ Were you responsible for the bird's care?
- ✔ What happened to that bird?
- ✔ What other animals live in your home?
- ✔ What parrot books have you read recently?
- ✔ Do you intend to maintain this bird as a companion or as a breeder?
- ✔ How often do you believe a bird should see a veterinarian?
- ✔ Are you willing to assume all responsibility for this bird?
- ✔ At what date are you prepared to assume responsibility for this bird?
- ✔ Can you think of additional considerations that might affect this adoption?

is stolen and include a provision for termination of the agreement by either party. Most consignment agreements will probably include an abandonment clause, in which the store is declared full guardian of the bird if it doesn't hear from you or if you cannot be found for a period of time.

Organizations

If ability to care for a bird has been suddenly eroded, then emergency placement through an adoption organization may be necessary. Many local and American Federation of Aviculture-affiliated clubs operate adoption placement programs. Most of these programs are run by volunteers and are free of charge, although the program may request a donation from both the person placing the bird for adoption and the person adopting the bird.

Macaws can outlive several caregivers. People who keep long-lived parrots need to make plans for their future homes.

The Quiet Human

Tom was a quiet young man. He came to parrot-care classes and sat in the back of the room. He seemed introverted and a little sad.

J. R. was a 26-year-old Double Yellow-headed Amazon who hated everyone and savagely bit any of the volunteers who tried to care for him. Because he was considered a difficult case, none of the volunteers with children or other birds wanted to foster him. Tom volunteered to try. Incredibly, J. R. stepped up for Tom without hesitation and went home with him.

In two weeks' time, everyone was astonished at the change in both bird and human! Tom was suddenly talking excitedly to everyone about all the great things J. R. would say and do. The cranky Amazon was now hanging upside down from Tom's index finger and openly showing his affection for the new person in his life. It was obvious to everyone that these two belonged together. Tom adopted J. R. and they continue to provide each other with love and companionship.

—Cathy Isbel

Additionally, adoption organizations have more experience evaluating people and homes for placement. Some organizations prescreen and maintain a list of qualified people seeking to adopt a parrot.

If there are no pressing problems related to the bird's care, it's probably best for the bird to stay in its present home rather than have to go to a foster home where quarantine and other flock issues might be complicated. Keep the bird until the adoption organization has found a suitable permanent home.

Documentation and Foster Homes

Some of the most bitter disputes and misunderstandings in the bird community have developed as a result of adoptions. Nowhere in aviculture is there a greater need for record keeping. If no other document is made, be sure to complete a written receipt or document transferring guardianship of the bird.

Documentation is also important in foster care. If no permanent home is available and the bird must be removed immediately from

A healthy African grey.

Be sure to keep accurate records throughout the process of adopting your bird.

its present home, then a temporary home must be provided. This can create many complications, as there is always a possibility of accident, illness, or other misfortune in the temporary home. Obtain a written agreement designating the duties and responsibilities of the temporary care provider. Be sure that it covers quarantine and specifies what happens if other birds in the home fall ill. A written agreement should also state the conditions under which foster care can be terminated by the temporary care provider, by the bird's guardian, or by the organization supervising the adoption.

Sanctuary

If a particular bird has been unsuccessful in adjusting to several homes and it seems likely to be bounced from home to home for the rest of its life, it might best be placed with a permanent sanctuary organization. For a placement of this type, look for an organization that has a chance for long-term survival. An organization that achieves and maintains 501 (c)(3) status, enabling it to accept tax-exempt donations, is probably more capable of this than most private individuals or adoption organizations that have not yet achieved this official designation. Because a 501 (c)(3) organization's tax forms are available for public examination, if you're truly motivated, you can determine how financially prepared for survival a particular organization is. As with any potential home, be selective. The quality of your bird's future life depends upon your choice.

Glossary

Please note that the following definitions set forth the meanings of these words as they are used specifically in this text. They are not intended to be full and complete definitions.

abandonment: separation from the perceived flock.

adoption: the process of assuming all responsibility for the care of a parrot.

aggression: hostile nipping, biting, or chasing.

apron: an accessory that protrudes from the lower portion of the cage and catches debris before it reaches the floor.

aviary birds: birds that live in captivity, but in a bird-identified setting in which they do not interact on a regular basis with humans.

behavior
    self-rewarding: an activity that is enacted solely for the pleasure of doing it.

bite: use of the parrot's beak in a manner intended to cause damage or injury.

bite zone: area in front of the bird's beak in which the hand can be more easily reached by the beak than the feet.

bond: an emotional or social attachment.

bonding: the connection with another bird, a human, object, or location that a bird exhibits and defends.

boredom: stress caused to a companion parrot by lack of access to activities that it would be instinctually suited to experience, including both interesting wild and self-rewarding companion pastimes.

breeding-related behaviors: behaviors with a source related to breeding habits in the wild such as chewing, emptying cavities, hiding in dark places, allopreening, allofeeding, masturbating, copulating, and aggression at the nest site (cage).

call: a redundant, routine, or presumed-to-be natural vocaliztion.

carrier: a device for protecting the bird as it is transported from place to place.

chewing: breeding-related behavior involving destruction of wood or other shredable environmental elements.

command: an order or instruction given by a dominant individual.

co-parent: a guardian who shares care responsibilities with another person or family.

covert: feathers that protect the bases and new growth of the long feathers of the wing.

dander: powder formed when discarded sheaths are removed from new feathers or powder that is contained in certain down feathers that is released when the bird preens.

developmental period: a period of rapid behavioral development wherein parrots may demonstrate tendencies for dominance, independence, aggression, and panic. See also: Terrible Twos.

down: the small fuzzy feathers next to the body that are normally covered by contours.

drama: any activity that brings an exciting response, either positive or negative.

droppings: the combination of urates, water, and fecal material excreted from the vent.

environment
    behavioral: behavioral conditions, especially redundant behaviors including habits, present in the bird and in individuals around the bird.

eye contact: maintaining eye-to-eye gaze.

fearfulness: the behavioral expression of fear.

feather

chewing: self-inflicted feather damage involving any part of the feather including the edges or the center shaft, or rachis.

picking: self-inflicted feather damage including shredding, snapping, or plucking feathers from the follicles.

plucking: pulling feathers from the follicles.

pulling: plucking feathers from the follicles.

shredding: self-inflicted damage to the edge of the barbs of the contour feathers, sometimes giving the feathers a hairlike appearance.

snapping: self-inflicted feather damage involving breaking the center shaft.

tracts: symmetrical lines on a bird's body where feathers grow in; especially visible on baby parrots.

feces: excreted solid waste, usually "wormlike," which can be differentiated from urates and liquid urine.

feral: previously captive animals living wild.

fight-or-flight response: instinctual, automatic reaction to real or perceived danger.

flock/flock members: as it applies to a companion bird, human companions sharing a home with a captive parrot.

grooming: the process of having the companion parrot's wing feathers trimmed, nails cut or filed, and beak shaped, if necessary.

guardian: a human who assumes all responsibility for care for another creature.

habit: redundant behavior that has become a fixed part of the bird's behavior.

hand-fed: a parrot that as a neonate was fed by humans rather than birds.

honeymoon period: a young parrot's first, impressionable weeks in the new home, an idyllic period before instinctual adult behavior develops.

hookbill: a parrot

human/mate: the human companion chosen by the bird to fill the role of mate; the bird will perform courtship displays and protect this person as it would a mate of the same species.

imperfect: a bird with an obvious physical defect resulting from congenital anomaly or injury.

independence: improvising and enjoying self-rewarding behaviors.

juvenile: fully weaned, but immature parrots. Also, behaviors unrelated to nesting or breeding.

keel bone: the flat bone below the bird's crop that is attached perpendicular to the sternum.

language: vocal communication wherein multiple individuals use the same groups of sounds to convey the same meaning.

language, body: nonvocal communication involving posturing, displaying, or otherwise signaling an individual's feelings or intentions

life span: reported longevity, presumed to represent the potential time a bird will live.

mandible: the lower beak or horny protuberance with which the bird bites against the inside of the maxilla.

mate: the individual to whom the parrot is primarily bonded. See also: human/mate.

maxilla: the upper beak; the notched protuberance that gives the hookbill its name.

mimic: to copy modeled behavior, especially vocalizations.

model: a learning process by which one individual copies behavior from another individual.

molt: the cyclical shedding and replacing of feathers.

mutilation, feather: self-induced damage to the feathers.

mutilation, self: self-induced damage to the skin.

naturalized: a non-native feral parrot that has learned to survive in the habitat into which it escaped.

neonate: a baby parrot that cannot yet sustain itself by eating food independently.

nest/nesting: the act of constructing a structure for the purpose of reproduction.

nest box: a human-constructed box for bird nesting.

nipping: accidental, unintentional, or non-aggressive pinch not intended to cause damage.

parrot: a hookbill; a bird with a notched maxilla, a mallet shaped tongue, and four toes (two facing front and two facing back).

breeder: a parrot that has lived with a supposed mate, whether or not they have produced offspring.

companion: a parrot that lives as a companion to humans.

second-hand: a companion parrot that has occupied two or more homes.

patterning: stimulating an individual to repeat behaviors through the process of repeatedly drilling the behavior.

pinch: a behavior designed to get a human's attention where the bird takes that person's skin in its beak and squeezes hard enough to cause pain, but not hard enough to break the skin.

play: to engage in self-rewarding behaviors

powder-coated: a hard, baked-on metal cage bar finish.

preen: to groom the feathers, as in "combing" and "zipping" them with the beak.

prompt: a cue, here used for the physical cue to cause the bird to step up.

psittacine: any parrot.

quarantine: enforced isolation for the prevention of disease transmission.

recapture: to apprehend or recover possession of a parrot that has flown away.

rehabilitate: special care intended to return a bird to health and well-being.

reinforce: process of rewarding a behavior that we wish to become habitual.

reprimand: punishment; action intended to discourage a behavior.

rescue: fortuitous removal from dangerous, frightening, substandard, or no-longer-available circumstances, including adopting into a more favorable home.

rival: a competitor, one who competes for territory, mate, food, reinforcement, or reward.

roost: the place where a bird usually sleeps.

sanctuary: a facility where birds live out their lives and are not adopted out.

scream: loud, raucous call.

sexual maturity: the period during which breeding-related behaviors become prominent in the bird's overall behavior.

shelter: a facility out of which birds are placed in new homes.

species: subgenus; related groups of individuals that share common biological characteristics.

socialize: to teach a parrot human-compatible behaviors.

step-up: practice of giving the *step-up* command with the expectation that the bird will perform the behavior.

stress: any stimulus, especially fear or pain, that inhibits normal psychological, physical, or behavioral balance.

tamed: a parrot that has learned, by abandoning previous aggression or fearfulness, to interact successfully with humans.

Terrible Twos: a behavioral period wherein the bird's instincts for dominance, independence, and aggression are first manifest. See also: developmental period

"thunderbolt": a parrot's tendency to be smitten by love at first sight.

tool: an implement that is manipulated to accomplish a particular function.

toxin: any substance that causes illness or death through exposure or consumption.

toy: any tool for producing self-rewarding behavior.

urates: nitrogenous wastes; the solid "white" part of a bird's excrement.

urine, liquid: clear, colorless liquid part of the bird's excrement.

vent: opening through which droppings are excreted.

Information

Other Books by These Authors

Athan, Mattie Sue. *Guide to a Well-Behaved Parrot.* Hauppauge, NY: Barron's Educational Series, Inc., 1999.

Athan, Mattie Sue. *Guide to Companion Parrot Behavior.* Hauppauge, NY: Barron's Educational Series, Inc., 1999.

Athan, Mattie Sue and Deter, Dianalee. *Guide to the Senegal Parrot and its Family.* Hauppauge, NY: Barron's Educational Series, Inc., 1998.

Athan, Mattie Sue and Deter, Dianalee. *The African Grey Parrot Handbook.* Hauppauge, NY: Barron's Educational Series, Inc., 2000.

Athan, Mattie Sue. *Guide to the Quaker Parrot.* Hauppauge, NY: Barron's Educational Series, Inc., 1997.

Organizations

American Holistic Veterinary Medical Association (AHVMA)
(410) 569-0795

Association of Avian Rescue Organizations (AARO)
(619) 287-9617

Association of Avian Veterinarians
(561) 393-8901
Fax (561) 393-8902

Videos

"Fantastic Performing Parrots," Robar Productions, 1994.

"Parrots: Look Who's Talking," Thirteen/WNET and BBC-TV, 1995.

"Spirits of the Rainforest," Discovery Communications, Inc., 1993.

"Vanishing Birds of the Amazon," Audubon Productions and Turner Original Productiona, 1996.

Web Sites

goodfeather.com: This site features general information on parrots, brief pieces on behavior, and "links to the best birds around."

positivelyparrots.com: This site contains useful information on parrot adoption, behavior, and grooming. Their motto is "Making life easier for parrots and their people."

quakerville.com: Dedicated entirely to the Quaker Parrot, this site contains links to health-care ideas, general information, and plenty of pictures and stories featuring Quakers.

About the Authors

Mattie Sue Athan has been studying companion parrot behavior since 1978. Her areas of special interest are the development of behavior in companion parrots and the effect of environment on companion parrot behavior. Her first book, *Guide to a Well-Behaved Parrot*, currently in its second edition, remains an industry standard almost a decade after its first publication. Mattie Sue also wrote *Guide to Companion Parrot Behavior* and *Guide to the Quaker Parrot*, and is currently working on *Parrots* for Barron's Pet Manual Series.

Dianalee Deter-Townsend has a Bachelor of Science degree in zoology from the University of Florida. She has been studying and finding homes for second-hand parrots since 1986. She breeds Amazons, macaws, African greys, Poicephalous, Quakers, and cockatiels. Dianalee owns Paradise Found, a bird store in Westminster, Colorado, where she lives with her husband, Rod, and their four children.

Mattie Sue Athan and Dianalee Deter-Townsend also co-authored *Guide to the Senegal Parrot and Its Family* and *The African Grey Parrot Handbook* for Barron's Educational Series.

Photo Credits

Mattie Sue Athan: 12 (bottom r), 13 (top), 17, 24 (top), 37, 44 (bottom), 53 (bottom), 57 (left), 61, 65, 73. Joan Balzarini: 9, 25. Dianalee Deter: 4, 12 (top l, top r), 13 (bottom), 20 (both), 21 (top), 24 (bottom), 32, 33 (all), 36, 40 (all), 41 (all), 44 (top l, top r), 48, 49, 52 (bottom), 56 (both), 57 (right), 60, 72, 76, 77, 80, 88. Susan Green: 5, 8, 9, 21 (bottom), 28, 29, 45 (all), 52 (top), 53 (top), 64, 68, 69, 81 (both), 84, 85. Lisa Lalone: 12 (bottom l). Matthew Vriends: 89 (both).

A Word of Warning

While every effort has been made to ensure that all information in this text is accurate, up-to-date, and easily understandable, we cannot be responsible for unforeseen consequences of the use or misuse of this information. Poorly socialized or unhealthy parrots may be a danger to humans in the household. Escaped non-native species represent an environmental threat in some places. Outdoor release or unrestricted outdoor flight is absolutely condemned by the ethical parrot keeper. This book recommends that a parrot's wing feathers be carefully trimmed at least three times a year.

Dedication

For my mother. (MSA)
To H, R, and J, and Sharon, Sue, Heidi, and Angie. (DD)

Acknowledgments

With special thanks to Mickey Muck, Dr. Paul Welch, Cathy Isbel, and Gale Whittington.

Cover Photos

Front: Joan Balzarini. Back: Susan Green. Inside front: Susan Green. Inside back: Joan Balzarini.

All inquiries should be addressed to:
Barron's Educational Series, Inc.
250 Wireless Boulevard
Hauppauge, NY 11788
http://www.barronseduc.com

International Standard Book No. 0-7641-1918-4

Library of Congress Catalog Card No. 2001043989

Library of Congress Cataloging-in-Publication Data
Athan, Mattie Sue.
    The second-hand parrot / Mattie Sue Athan and Dianalee Deter-Townsend.
        p. cm.
    ISBN 0-7641-1918-4
        1. Parrots. 2. Animal rescue. I. Deter-Townsend, Dianalee. II. Title

SF473.P3 A85   2002
636.6'865—dc21   2001043989

Printed in China

9 8 7 6 5 4